Straight, NO CHASER

ALSO BY JILL NELSON

Volunteer Slavery

HOW I BECAME A
GROWN-UP BLACK WOMAN

Straight,

NO CHASER

JILL NELSON

G. P. PUTNAM'S SONS
NEW YORK

G. P. Putnam's Sons
Publishers Since 1838
a member of
Penguin Putnam Inc.
200 Madison Avenue
New York, NY 10016

Library of Congress Cataloging-in-Publication Data

Nelson, Jill, date.
Straight, no chaser : how I became a grown-up black woman / Jill Nelson.
p.   cm.
ISBN 0-399-14262-2 (alk. paper)
1. Nelson, Jill.   2. Afro-American journalists—
Washington, D.C.—Biography.   3. Afro-American women—Washington,
D.C.—Biography.   I. Title.
PN4874.N295A3   1997   97-14596 CIP
070'.92—dc21
[B]

Printed in the United States of America
5   7   9   10   8   6   4

This book is printed on acid-free paper. ♾

Book design by June Lee

For Aunt Florence, mostly silent
For Deletha Word, who was silenced
And for all my sisters who still have voice

CONTENTS

ACKNOWLEDGMENTS

THIS BOOK WAS NURTURED by friends, family, and many women, living and dead, known and unknown, whose lives touched mine during the process of writing it. I thank all those who remembered, understood, argued, laughed, and encouraged me. Special thanks to my readers, women and men, who both challenged and supported me. Especially Valerie Wilson Wesley.

Thanks also to E. Stacy Creamer, my editor, who fought for this book, my agent, Faith Hampton Childs, who once again persevered, Arlene Stoltz and Emily Bernard, who went far beyond what was expected, and my daughter, Misumbo, who reminds me every day what is at stake.

The woman was struggling and fighting like a tiger all the time, but the mob was too much for her, and a minute later she was swinging in the air, with her feet several inches from the ground. All of a sudden she twisted around and grabbed a man by the collar, jerked a knife from his hands and cut the rope that was choking the life out of her.

(Article in *The Louisville Courier-Journal* on the attempted lynching of a black woman, Marie Thompson, in Statesboro, Georgia, 1904; *From Slavery to Freedom,* by John Hope Franklin and Alfred A. Moss, Jr.)

ONCE, NOT ALL THAT LONG AGO, I thought that I was alone. And invisible. And crazy. Thought I was the only black woman who woke up feeling assaulted by being black and female in America. The only sister shuddering under the weight of being a woman of African descent trapped in the negative context of belonging to the two most loathed groups in America, those who are black and those who are female. Thought I was the only one who wanted to scream and lash out, and sometimes did, under the pressure of work and children and family, men and community. I thought there was something wrong with me, that everyone else was living happily ever after while I could find no center of power. Then I started to watch, listen, and talk about how I felt to other black women. Casually in living rooms, on the telephone, in the grocery store, in passing on the street, at meetings. I saw, heard, and felt my reflection in them and theirs in me. Now, it is impossible to feel alone, or invisible, or crazy for long. I have a whole nation of sisters with me. The question is how do we connect, turn our similar lives and shared concerns into action?

There is among black women a commonality of experience, attitude, and world view. But it is most often a veiled, quiet unity. Unlike white men we do not have most of the political power and nearly all of the corporate money. Unlike white women we are neither the wives nor sisters of the masters of the universe. We have no National Organization for Women or other group with clout to advocate for us. Even though black women do most of the work in our communities, are the mainstay of the strongest organization African Americans have, the black church, unlike black men we seldom head churches, are elected to political office, are in leadership. Black women are an enormous, disorganized army of hardworking sisters without collective organization, voice, or agenda. But the ties of race and gender, the basic ties of the color of our skin and the fact that we are women, bind us to one another. They are strong, these ties, made up of our rage at the situations in which we exist, our potential for love, and our hope for the future. Such ties, understood, re-created, and used strategically, need not oppress us, but could be used not only to liberate black women, but to transform the culture in which we live.

I want to write the true story of what it is like to be a black woman growing up and living in America, and African America, to fight the invisibility and erasure that too often defines being black and female in America. Ours is a story that is seldom told, and most often when it is it is fictionalized, as if we all subconsciously recognize that no one wants to hear, see, read, or publish our true stories. Instead, what we get are distorted, fictionalized representations of our loneliness and our rage. Reading popular fiction, most times you'd think the only desire, answer, and alternative for a black woman is to find a man. Barring that, we have the choice of committing suicide, homicide, or going slowly crazy. Occasionally, a book of essays or an academic treatise on black women will appear. But too often it is as if we are an alien species being examined under a microscope in order to fulfill some scholar's requirement that they "publish or perish" in order to gain tenure. We are distant subjects to be studied to prove a thesis, usually negative: that we give birth to children carelessly, are bad parents, overbearing matriarchs, a burden on America's social service system, emasculators of black men. Our fundamental woman-ness is erased by the rhetoric and political agenda of whoever's writing about us. Instead, we become archetypes or icons, alienated from the larger community of women and women's experience that crosses race, age, and class. Most of the time it is not myself nor any recognizable woman I see in that mirror, but a distorted reflection of a woman who maybe, once, kinda sorta looked like me.

I want to write about black women because I know that I am neither a fictionalized archetype nor a nonfiction representative of a pathology, trend, or larger problem. I have also learned that if I don't speak up for myself and other black women, by my silence I acquiesce to the definitions of others, and there are plenty of them. Sometimes it seems as if everyone wants a piece of me to use for their own—usually negative—purposes. White male politicians demonize me as a welfare cheat, illegitimate baby–making machine, and drain on government programs. White feminist women ignore me, cut deals for themselves, and then invite me to the meeting, panel, or forum as an afterthought, when it suddenly occurs to them that they need a visible—and preferably silent—black woman on stage to give their self-interested agenda the image of inclusion. Black men single me out when they need either help or an example of why they are "endangered" or hindered. I am asked to cook the food, stuff the envelopes, open my legs, and keep my mouth shut. Failing to do these things, I am blamed for black men's ineffectiveness.

But the truth is, horrible as these ways in which black women are distorted and exploited by others are, most of the time people like me are simply invisible. No one notices or thinks or writes about our needs, our lives, the events that made us who we are and who we might in our dreams aspire to become. We simply do not matter except in the ways we relate to and reflect those who are not, like us, black and female. Most of the time that relationship is a negative one. We are the poor black woman who, depending on whose use she's being put to, needs too much help, deserves some help, or isn't helpful enough.

I want to write about black women to enable us to take voice, center stage, put us into the private and public dialogue which often has a devastating effect on our lives and from which we are usually excluded. I don't want to pimp black women because that would be the same as prostituting myself. I just want to get myself and my sisters into the discussion, join the fray. The singer Chaka Khan had a hit song in the early 1980s. The first line went, "I'm every woman, it's all in me." There's a collective consciousness among black women. It is not that we are all the same, just composed of many similar pieces, connected across class and age. I want to write about some of the crucial events in my own life as a way of identifying common threads in the lives of women, particularly black women. Once we've picked up those threads, I want to join the process of quilting, pulling those pieces together into whole cloth that will protect, shelter, and speak for all of us.

I write because I'm angry. Angry at either being ignored or defined and spoken for by others. According to many politicians, all the social ills black women are supposedly responsible for—drain on welfare and Medicaid, producers of illegitimate, violent children, the decline of civility—would disappear if we'd just get married, serve our man, and fit into the nuclear family program, marriage as the solution to America's problems. Too many white feminists seem to think that gender and men are the sum total of the problem, that if black women would just abandon black men, see them for the brutish, loser cads they are, we could ascend to some feminist nirvana, in which the only thing threatening us would be the glass ceiling. Sad to say, these days too many black men seem to think we're the problem: We're stealing their jobs, too assertive, ball-busters. We need to get back behind Big Daddy and stay there.

But the truth is that the ills of white men, white women, or black men are not black women's fault or responsibility. We are all living in what I believe is a dying white culture here in America. You can yearn as much as you'd like for Elvis, the Brady Bunch, Jell-O molds, "American Bandstand," "I Like Ike," and separate but equal, but the truth is those things are gone, over, done, relegated to the realm of nostalgia. But we have yet to come to any agreement about what will replace the dying white culture. What is obvious is that many of the fundamental values upon which this country was founded are no longer powerful, believable, or functional. Whatever your politics, we are all wrestling with the challenge to white supremacy by the browning of America by immigrants of color, with the reality that the economic assumption that everyone who wanted to work would find a job is no longer realistic, that men's and women's roles are changing, and that the structure and function of marriage and family is constantly mutating, that the violence which America has wreaked upon the world has now come home to roost. So far, the political and social response has been overwhelmingly mean-spirited. We look to blame the women, the immigrants, the poor, black men. This is not surprising, since the death of a culture and its fundamental assumptions is frightening and overwhelming, both for those most included in that culture and those who survive on its edges. As a black woman, I am afraid of what I see happening around me, but I am more terrified by what sort of society we will end up with if I do not speak up, get involved, gain voice. I know this fear is a fundamental part of the road to transformation. I also know that road presents the only possibility of creating an alternative, more equitable, egalitarian society.

But too frequently, the fear that somehow our specific group will be excluded from or have less in a changed society dominates. In response to these cultural earthquakes, people look around for someone to blame, as if assigning responsibility for the sometimes frightening ways the culture is changing will somehow ease the pain or stop the momentum. White men attempt to shore up a bursting dam by reasserting their supremacy and divine right as patriarchs and leaders of the free world while the rest of us scramble for a piece of the pie, whatever crumbs they might drop, but most of the time simply survive, keep our heads above water. Like those old crabs in a barrel, we do this by climbing on someone else's back for leverage. Black women are at the bottom of this frantic pyramid of survivalists.

This is where we are placed, and it is sometimes where we place ourselves, at the bottom and last. Black women are the ones with our feet on the earth, who always hit the ground running. We work jobs, take care of children, elderly relatives, the church, community organizations, and, in various ways, black men. Most of us go to work every day at crummy, unrewarding jobs at low wages and even less respect. We come home to communities devastated by unemployment and the drugs and violence that are its handmaidens, praying that we make it safely to our houses from the subway, bus stop, or car. Once home, it does not matter if we are exhausted. We cook, clean, help with homework, soothe the battered egos of our men, make love, check on those who do not live with us, yet to and for whom we are responsible. We fall into bed with a dozen chores still undone, too tired to take a long bath, or read, or do our nails, or just steal a few moments to think about ourselves. Then it's morning, time to start all over again.

After a while, we get so used to working all the time to care for others that we come to think ourselves undeserving of care. No one around us offers assistance or says, "Take some time for yourself." The culture that we consume through television, magazines, and advertisements confirms our lack of importance. We are totally absent from all serious political discussion. Even during February, Black History Month, black men are the preferred race representatives. March, Women's History Month, is for white women only. We might get occasional play in the news, but most frequently as someone causing problems, asking for too much, or occasionally, Super Victimizer, as in "Crack Smoking Mom Beats Toddler to Death." Entertainment? Forget it. Even though black Americans watch more free network television than anyone else, there is not a single dramatic show on television about black women, much less a black woman producing one. When it comes to beauty, the preoccupation of women's magazines and women's programming, we are definitely not up to snuff. We're too dark, big-boned, our features too Negroid, too ethnic-looking, in short, too much black women, to even qualify to enter America's beauty sweepstakes. Still, it's the only game in town, so we try and fit in. Our hair is too short and nappy, so we pay big money to have yards of synthetic hair woven in. Is it my imagination, or is black women's collective national hairline receding from the weight of extensions and hair weaves? We starve ourselves, compulsively buy new and supposedly better things with which to adorn ourselves, search for affirmation through the status of the men we are with. Still, when we look in the mirror it's hard to put on a happy face, since no matter what we do we remain who we are, black women in America, invisible at worst, unattractive at best. What would make us seize the time to care for and love ourselves when most of the signals we get from everyone not like us, and sadly, from those who are like us, tells us we are undeserving and undesirable? When was the last time you saw a black male public figure with a brown or dark-skinned wife whose hair wasn't conked or woven?

Even so, we always think that we can "fix it," all-suffering, all-sacrificing Superwomen that we've been told we are. Most of us never find the time to stop and realize that believing we can and should fix everything presupposes that we're responsible for breaking it in the first place. We're not. Believing we are dooms us to failure, since the first thing we have to fix is ourselves, and most black women are so busy helping everyone else, we never even get around to that.

The affirmation, strength, and voice that black women desperately need must initially come from ourselves and other black women, those who share our experiences. It's crucial that we have unity with ourselves and each other, that black women learn to listen to, respect, and place value on black women, before we can emerge as strong voices and forces in the complex political and cultural climate in which we live. We need to first begin talking to each other and then to those who are not like us, black men, white women, and anyone else, so that we can begin to draw an honest, self-defined notion of who we are into the picture and the dialogue. Those who don't define themselves are doomed to be defined by others, erased, or, as is the case with black women, both. This book is about talking about some of those experiences we've all had and connecting the dots, drawing a picture of who we are, how we became who we are, thinking collectively about who we'd like to be next. About what being a black woman really requires, and it has nothing to do with playing with dolls or having babies. About learning as a girl that women just aren't as important as men and Daddy has all the power, then growing up to find out the same thing's still true and figuring out how to fight it. About understanding that you'd be hard-pressed to find one woman in a room of hundreds who hasn't been physically or verbally abused by a man, and accepting that you really didn't "ask for it." About the dizzying speed with which a woman can go from being middle class to being poor, on welfare, and alone. About how Ronald Reagan and the right wing set the tone for reformulating America by first attacking black women, and most people didn't care until their program started to roll on them and was in full swing. And it's about wanting to love and be loved in a very bad situation and figuring out how to do that. Most of all, I hope this book is a public way for us to begin to own our experience, turn our rage into action, take collective voice, and enter the battle. In order to do that, I have to tell some secrets.

Not long ago, a black woman told me that she didn't think I should write about my life, and particularly sex, because, "What do you think a white man is going to think about you and black women when he reads this? How could you write something like this for white men to read?"

I think about this question frequently, troubled by her concern about what Mr. Anonymous White Man might think about my life in particular and, by extension, all black women. That is not my concern or interest. Yet I know that her concern is one that dominates the lives of black people in America. We have an inordinate investment in what white folks think about us, how we appear to them. We have a collective obsession with fronting and posturing for white people, not airing dirty laundry, which frequently comes down to not facing or dealing with reality. Whether we're talking about a book, movie, political leader, elected official, or community crisis, too often maintaining the illusion that we have our act together for the benefit of white people takes precedence over honestly looking at and critiquing what's going on. This is a total waste of time. The fact is that all the individual and collective energy we spend posturing would be much better spent in activism, re-creating ourselves, our communities, and this nation as we would like it to be, an equitable, humane, and safe place for all of us, instead of maintaining the delusion that everything's all right. The truth is that except in cases of emergency and necessity—generally defined as crime, drugs, or too much government spending—most of the time white people aren't thinking about black people at all. Even when they are they'd prefer not to.

Black people are big on keeping race secrets. It's as if the bond of our skin color demands that we keep up at least a facade of monolithic solidarity, even when doing so cripples and disenfranchises us. This is compounded when it comes to black women, since in our communities the bonds of race do not extend across gender, and if we are insane or brainwashed-by-whitey enough to believe we are oppressed because we are women as well, we'd best keep that belief a gender secret. More often than not women are attacked or dismissed if we center our identity in our femaleness. The men are always more important than the women, and, when it comes to issues particular to women, there's not much difference between a black or white patriarch. One of the few arenas in a racist, patriarchal society where black men are legitimately allowed to wield power is over black women.

As a people we have a collective inferiority complex, one of the emotional and psychological effects of slavery and its aftermath. We've bought into white people's line that they are inherently better, conferred perfect status on that which is white, and automatically negated ourselves. Our standard has become "Am I as good as this or that white person?" and "What will anonymous white person think?" Not only does this presuppose the superiority and goodness of that which is white, it also absolves us of responsibility for creating standards, systems, and values for ourselves: We just use white people's. Is it any wonder so many of us are stressed out, angry, and self-hating?

This keeping of secrets operates in every area of our lives. As families, we avoid talking about that which is difficult. Marriages, break-ups, values, how someone really feels—all are off limits in most families. We superimpose the construct of the typical American family, à la "Leave It to Beaver" and "The Brady Bunch," over our very different lives and, like the wicked stepsisters and that shoe in Cinderella, try and make it fit. We may be bloodied, hobbling, and in excruciating economic, political, and psychic pain, but we're determined to go to the ball. As partners we mimic the idealized rituals and structure of the patriarchal, nuclear family, deny that it is a terrible design and fit, and refuse to go about the crucial business of creating workable, alternative structures, ones that take into account economic reality, social needs, and the statistical unavailability of black men. In our communities we have forgotten the interwoven sense of individual and collective responsibility that helped us survive, succeed, and excel prior to integration.

Black folks' saving grace used to be that our standards for ourselves and each other were higher than white people's and everyone else's. They had to be in order to survive, succeed, and not go berserk in America. As slaves, we hid our African religions under the liturgy and symbols of Christianity and sustained our faith. We trudged to heatless, segregated schools with outmoded textbooks, grabbed an education, and excelled. We allowed segregationists to beat us brutally during the civil rights movement and consistently turned the other cheek, confident that eventually America's moral conscience would kick in. Whether it was going to the fields to slave, or polls to try and register to vote, or to universities or jobs that did not want us, wrote us off as substandard affirmative action placements, we carried ourselves with confidence and dignity, stood for what we believed was right. That sense of greater mission and expectation, of individual and community responsibility, is almost extinct. I'm not one of those believers in "the worst thing that ever happened to black people was integration," but it's important to remember it's a process, not something declared. I think too many people thought the struggle was over when they saw black representations in the mass culture, on television, T-shirts, and advertisements, as if visual representations meant we were free at last. In addition, the attack by a greedy right wing panicked by the inevitable shrinking of American resources, and the new American mantra, "Everything that's wrong is the fault of those demanding, ill-behaved, expensive Negroes," has exacerbated the problem. In ways large and small we've relinquished most of the fundamental notion of community and collectivity that were responsible for both our endurance and achievement. Nowadays, the greatest threat to the lives of black men are other black men, the greatest violence visited on black women is by black men, the candy store is a bulletproof, Plexiglas fortress from which sweets are dispensed not by a human hand but on a lazy Susan, and if you see a man go to the curb and spit he's probably over forty, since the current etiquette is to spit on the sidewalk in front of yourself and then walk in it. This says something casually, devastatingly negative about the contempt in which people hold their communities and themselves. As for not being a litterbug? You'd be hard-pressed to find a kid today who knows what one is. A few months ago I cracked on a boy of eight or nine who threw a candy wrapper on the sidewalk, and he looked at me as if I was speaking in tongues. When I explained to him what a litterbug was, he did pick up the paper. Then he scampered away from me like I was crazy.

As Americans, we have become cynical, a cynicism whose effect is most profound among those most excluded. Black Americans are no longer, as Martin Luther King, Jr. described us, "the moral conscience of the nation." Black elected officials, whose right to vote and run for office are the result of the civil rights movement and whose mandate once came from a sense of collective good, now lie, steal, and fornicate with regularity. When busted, their response is to lie. When confronted with irrefutable evidence, they point fingers at others, usually white, who commit the same crimes, as if suddenly two wrongs do make a right or the playing field was miraculously leveled. We keep silent while we are pimped and bilked by black politicians, as if it's somehow okay because at least it's a black face ripping us off. There was a time when we looked on the rotten economic, political, and social pie of America and said, "Let us work for transformation." Nowadays, we've become so hopeless and despairing that we help ourselves to the largest slice of rancid pie we can get.

Our leaders, and I use that term with trepidation, are by and large useless opportunists, profoundly out of touch with the lives of those they allegedly represent. Still, for the most part, we keep their race secrets, do not call them out on their reactionary politics, their conservatism, their ignorance, their oppression of women, their tricksterism and glaring personal flaws. In fact, when someone—usually white media or black women—dares to criticize them, we attack the messenger, studiously avoiding the message.

It's not only black people who have secrets. As Americans, we have massive, historical secrets. I read the history of the decades I have lived in and, with very few exceptions, see no glimmer of myself or people I knew. In the current climate of the right wing, Bill Clinton is defined by Newt Gingrich as representing "the counter-culture," when the truth is those who were truly counter-culture wouldn't have given Bill Clinton the time of day. The right wing, joined by bitter, disillusioned liberals turned neo-conservatives, have conspired to reduce the movements for social change of the 1960s to a fashion statement: bell bottoms, wedgies, tie-dyed fabric, and Afros. In the typical American rush to turn everything—including people, ideas, and social movements—into something that can be minimized, packaged, and sold, a process that tends to render things harmless, the real people, seismic upheavals, and lasting changes effected by everyday people over the last decades and every day are either forgotten, buried, or obscured. Hell, you'd think if you weren't Martin Luther King, Jr., Malcolm X, or an angry, threatening, rioting Negro trotting down the street with a refrigerator strapped to your back and a bottle of bourbon in each hand, you barely existed in the 60s. If you were a woman, of any color, you could either be Angela Davis for a moment in the 1970s, or a bra-burning-dyke-bitch for a few seconds during the Miss America pageant of 1968 in Atlantic City. The 1980s? We'd damned near disappeared by then, except as beyond rehabilitation, lock-them-up-for-life Willie Horton types or baby-making, cheating welfare queens à la Reagan and Bush, or capitalist success stories in blackface. Forget the thousands of ordinary people who fought for abortion rights, or against police violence, or for the end of apartheid, or for national health care. In the 90s, we're nothing but trouble: a burden on the federal, local, and state government, affirmative action whiners, people to be cut along with programs, more trouble than we're worth, which wasn't much to start with.

The civil rights movement, the sexual revolution, the Black

Panthers, women's liberation, the war in Vietnam, abortion rights, the Black Liberation Movement, cultural nationalism, gay liberation, like so many of my generation I was swept up in the movements for social change in the 1960s and 70s. Young and invulnerable, I lived in the moment, followed the hippie credo to Be Here Now. It has taken me and many others the last twenty years to begin to figure out what went wrong, to understand the connection between the events of 1968, the assassination of King, the police attack on anti-war activists at the Days of Rage at the Democratic Convention in Chicago, the murder by police of three black students on the campus of Jackson State (overshadowed by the shooting several weeks later of white students at Ohio's Kent State), the disappearance of marijuana from the streets of the black community and its replacement by heroin, and the election in 1980 of Ronald Reagan, so-called great communicator and standard bearer of the return of white male patriarchy. The election of Richard Milhous Nixon in 1968 was a collective shock to the system of black Americans, given Nixon's law and order rhetoric, his emphasis on "crime in the streets," and his focus on a "silent majority" whose unheard voices Nixon the clairvoyant deemed more important than those already raised in the struggle for social justice. Yet in hindsight it's easy to see Nixon's election as the cornerstone in a new wave of national scapegoating of black Americans—as opposed to social inequity—as the real cause of most of America's problems, a structure built upon by Reagan, Bush, and Clinton.

The truth is that the decades I have lived in have been shaped by ordinary people doing extraordinary things, the everyday people that most of us are, many of them black women. It is easy to forget or never know this. America makes stars out of a few—usually male—individuals and exhalts them to unattainable heights in the name of celebrating their contributions, when what this elevation to the status of icon actually does is disempower those of us still earth-bound. And that is where women, particularly women of color, usually are: on the ground, our feet covered with earth, taking care of business. We are left to stand in the dirt, crooks in our necks from trying to look up and catch a glimpse of our heroes, feeling unimportant, inadequate, and powerless. Waiting for the next leader to descend from above. The truth is each of us is the leadership, and as much as changes were made by those whom we call heroes, they were made even more by everyday people who lived quiet lives, often as second-class citizens, softly went about their business, and, when asked, stood for what was right. There was a revolution toward the left in the 1960s and early 1970s, the movement is right in the 1980s and 1990s. Too many of us have been paid, or bought, or pushed to the edges of the discussion—a place where our voices cannot reach the center, and go unheard—or have been simply beaten into complacency, apathy, forgetfulness, silence. But we are awakening. Our children have woken us up. With their rage, their violence, their questions, their needs. It's time we started talking.

It is essential that black women have a loud voice in the dialogue. Without the vibrant participation of black women, black people are assured of repeating the same failures that have historically crippled movements for social change. There can be no true transformation based on the exclusion or diminution of women's involvement. Black women are at this moment so far on the sidelines we can barely hear and are never heard in the political, social, and cultural debate. If we are mentioned, it is usually by opportunistic politicians as part of a catch-all of scary statistics designed to frighten the electorate into supporting the right wing. If an individual black woman does emerge, she's at best an entertainer, but more likely functions as a demonized representative of an enor-

mous problem requiring drastic measures: "reform" welfare, eliminate affirmative action, cut funds for education and day care, pass a
heinous crime bill, and build more prisons, one of the few growth
industries directed at people of color. The result of black women's
silence in the face of the verbiage of others is we find ourselves further misrepresented, erased, excluded. Those who demonize us and
call for cuts are usually white men who do not know a single black
woman. If they do, she's probably a domestic employee.

Black women have few representatives, no collective voice, no
power. Our communities are in a shambles, too many of our children are despairing and out of control. Our daughters think a big
butt and a baby makes them women, our sons that a penis and a
gun makes them men. Too many of my brothers are frustrated patriarch wannabes who take their anger out on women. The rising
right wing's rollback of government, with its segregationist-in-
conservative's-clothing cries for "states' rights," signals our erasure.
Still, we continue in a massive, collective orgy of fronting—pretending everything is all right for the benefit of everyone but ourselves. This is truly suicidal at a time when the president, the House,
and the Senate are committed to our further erasure. To stay silent
and keep race or gender or American secrets is to aid and abet my
own erasure. It is crucial that black women begin to speak up and
out, to speak the truth about what is really happening in ourselves,
our communities, and the larger culture. To begin discussing how
we implement the process of transformation, not only of the self
but the society.

This book is about telling secrets, talking honestly about our
history, our lives, the events, large and small, that made us who we
are, forced me to become a grown-up black woman. It is an effort
to speak openly about things that black women mostly don't talk
about, and certainly not in public, where Mr. Anonymous White

Man might hear us. Or we might upset the opportunist's apple cart by challenging the currently popular version of American history, or, if we are women, might reveal ourselves as independent, or feminist, or, if we are black women, niggerbitches, and will bring the race down, won't get our man, live happily ever after. It is an effort to start a dialogue. What is most important is that we own and acknowledge who we are and how we got to be here. Then we can begin the crucial and fascinating work of figuring out where we want to go and how to get there. It is time for us to place ourselves and our concerns in the center.

There is one thing I know for sure: secrets are not healthy, they are always more trouble than they are worth. The act of keeping secrets eventually becomes all-consuming: the initial secret spawns lies created in order to protect the secret, which spawns bigger and more dangerous lies, and more secrets. By its very nature, the keeping of secrets presupposes the greater importance of those from whom the secrets are being kept, whoever they are. All the energy black women could and should spend transforming self and community and this nation is instead spent maintaining secrets, self-mutilation and victimization at its insidious best. In letting the secrets out, black women place ourselves in the center. Secrets, I have learned, gain power not in the telling, but in the keeping.

Keep the faith, but not the secrets.

"YOU WANT TO DO WHAT?" My mother turns from the kitchen table where she is sitting snapping string beans. It is the spring of 1959. I am seven.

"Work for Betty Crocker," I say. From outside, just below where we live on Riverside Drive in Harlem, the horn of a tugboat pulling a barge up the Hudson River punctuates my sentence, puncturing my confidence.

"Betty Crocker?" My mother says the name as though she's never heard it before. The syllables roll off her tongue like words of a foreign language she's never spoken: it makes no sense to her.

"The cake mix lady," I prompt. I know my mother knows who I'm talking about, she buys cake mixes sometimes as a quick treat for the four of us. Otherwise, my mother is truly the scratch cake queen. The queen gives the royal nod, gazes out the window at the river passing by.

"Those are some bad cakes," she says finally, shaking her head and turning back to her beans. "Easy, but they have a bitter aftertaste. I can't figure out what it is . . ." Her voice and mind float away like the river, in search of that damn aftertaste. I want to stomp my foot, bang on the table, make those South Carolina string beans become Mexican jumping beans and dance in the colander, get my mother's attention from that aftertaste, those beans, onto me.

"I don't want to eat them. I want to bake them. For television." I say the last word slowly, with emphasis on each syllable, as if the fact that I'll be doing it on television makes my first career aspiration at least understandable, if not noble. In 1959, television is still relatively new, still fascinating. I think there is something adventurous about being on television, kind of like going into outer space. It will be quite a few years before it is public knowledge that the sole purpose of television is to sell things. Maybe that puts me in the vanguard.

My mother snaps a few more beans, lights a Viceroy cigarette.

"Why?" She looks me full in the face, her expression incredulous. "Why would you want to do that?" She says this as if I've said I want to work in a morgue. Not that there's anything wrong with working in a morgue, someone has to do it, it's honorable work, just not suitable for her youngest daughter. Or oldest daughter, middle son, baby boy.

"They're perfect," I say. "I know I could do it." My mother looks at me, the smile in her eyes traveling toward her mouth. Maybe she sees I'm serious, because the smile doesn't reach her lips.

"All right. If you say so," she says vaguely. I hug her neck, inhale her bittersweet odor of cigarette smoke and perfume. "Did you finish your homework?"

"All but the arithmetic."

"Go on and finish before dinner." My mother, back to decapitating beans, stares at the river passing by.

"Who needs math to bake cakes?" Visions of myself handing perfectly iced layer cakes to Betty moments before she goes into the little television box, the chocolate frosting thick with swirls, peaks, many hills and hardly any valleys, dance in my head. When the commercial's over, I wonder, do I get to eat my work?

"Who knows? It might come in handy." My mother shrugs. "Maybe you'll change your mind and decide to be a mathematician."

This is the earliest career aspiration I can recall. I did not want to be Betty Crocker herself, but Betty's baker. I wish my choice was motivated solely by my love of food, or baking, or helping others, but this would only be partially true. I think that even coming from a middle-class family of affirming, ambitious, successful people, it had already been communicated to me through the culture around me that as a black female, I was essentially invisible. Subconsciously, I chose a profession that confirmed my unseen place in society.

But I did not understand this then. In the beginning, in the house of my mother and father, I saw myself everywhere. In my sister and two brothers, in the care and attention of my mother and the expectations of my father, in the experiences and privileges they struggled to provide us. I did not suspect that as I grew older, left their protection, I would have to fight to remain visible and be seen as I saw myself, although now when I think about it, there were many signs that this was the case, that attempts at erasure were what awaited me, I just did not know how to read them. Too, my parents, being good, loving, hopeful, and successful, told the four of us that we were visible, important, that life would be different and wonderful for us. And they did not lie completely, we sometimes are and it sometimes is. But what my father could not and, I surmise, my mother would not tell my sister and me is that as we grew older, ventured out into the world, left home and entered the world of white people and the world of men, as black women our entitlement to visibility would come under direct assault. I believe that my mother knew these things. The challenge was how to tell her daughters about the barriers that awaited us without making us feel hopeless and inferior.

My father could not tell us about the limitations of gender because he did not know them, and there was no need for him to tell my sister Lynn and me much. We were his daughters, I was his baby girl, and it was enough that we were pretty and smart and well behaved, that we represented him well. My older and younger brothers were truly important to him. It was to them, Stanley and Ralph, he told things because they were, like him, male. My mother, an educated, funny, vibrant woman, stifled her own career as a businesswoman and subsequently a librarian for love of my father and at his behest, functioned instead as his wife, mother of his children, keeper of his house. My mother did not complain and she appeared to be at peace with her choices. I realize now that the signs of her discontent were present in her aloofness, her tense cigarette smoking, her joy when she packed her bags to travel alone to Indiana for a meeting of the hair care business of which she was president, a position that came to her because her father was the company attorney. In the loving, casual parenting that she showed toward the four of us when my father was not home. Indirectly, she told me and my sister about the possibility of erasure in her high academic expectations, in forcing us to read all the time, in talking to us about what we wanted to be when we grew up and never mentioning getting married or having children, in always pushing us to not necessarily do the girl thing. If, immersed in reading the series of "Cherry Ames" books, we said we wanted to be a nurse, my mother asked,

"Why not a doctor?" If the preferred profession of the moment was the glamorized 1950s vision of being an airline stewardess, complete with chic uniform and jaunty cap, my mother responded, "That's nothing but a flying maid. Wouldn't you rather be the pilot?" When I went through a phase of wanting to be an actress, my mother suggested I be a writer. In her quiet way, she pushed her two girls toward work that would afford us independence and visibility, knowing that she had conceded much of hers.

Although they talked to us about racism often, my parents methodically sheltered the four of us from the personal experience of it, and they were able, for many years, in the protected and proscribed world they created, to define being black solely as a positive experience. No one ever addressed me by a racial epithet. It wasn't until after desegregation of public facilities that I learned that the reason we didn't stop at gas stations on overnight drives—my father instead pulling to the side of the road, my mother opening both front and back doors to form a makeshift toilet stall, waking us in the back seat in our thin summer pajamas and pushing us outside to squat and pee before we drove on—was because there were no rest rooms available to black Americans.

If I was troubled as a child, it was about how to be female, a girl, a woman. The ambivalence I sensed in my mother's acquiescence to my father, the perception that there were feelings, ideas, and words kept neatly checked just beneath her surface, coupled with the lack of images of black women in popular culture, conspired to confuse me.

When I am young, many of the girls in my class want to be ballerinas, but I don't enjoy ballet class. Already I can see that I will never look fabulous in pink tights and a tutu, never have that frail, long-necked, I-can-see-the-blue-veins-under-the-skin look dancers have. It will be several years before the Alvin Ailey and Arthur Mitchell dance companies burst upon the scene and into the consciousness of little black girls with troupes filled with big-thighed, high-assed brown women who fly through the air with the greatest of ease. Some of my girlfriends want to be brides when they grow up, but it is clear that my parents have greater expectations than simply marriage. I cannot figure out what brides actually do after their wedding day. No one ever says, which leads me to suspect they don't do anything for a while and then become mothers. In third grade when we study Indians I decide I'd love to be a Native woman of the plains with an understanding of the land, a papoose, and a tipi. But when we get to the part about the blankets infected with smallpox virus and Wounded Knee, broken treaties, free alcohol, and reservations, I don't want to be a Native American anymore, unless I can go back and change the past.

As for the pioneer women, it seems to me they do all the dull, routine work that keeps everyone alive and safe, but never have any fun. The pioneer women live in cramped, cold, smoky log cabins and spend a lot of their time being scared of either the Indians or drunken, sex-starved male pioneers.

The room I share with my sister is filled with dolls. Dolls from around the world, rag dolls, Japanese dolls in kimonos, Native American dolls in beads and buckskin, Dutch dolls wearing tiny painted wooden shoes. The truth is that I never liked dolls, instead found them frightening and sinister, plastic bodies little girls were told to mother and pretend we loved. Dolls did not reflect me, either what I looked like or who I wanted to become. Still, I coveted them because everyone else did, and I thought I was supposed to. My loathing manifested in the way in which I played with them, especially the pink rubber baby dolls. After school my friends and I twist off arms and legs, cut open chest cavities in search of the voice box, stick pins in the behind of a peeing doll to see if we could make its bowels move. We drew on their faces, hacked off their hair, applied finger- and toenail polish, stuck arms into leg holes, created custom-made doll monsters.

I absorb suggestions from television, books, and the culture around me about who I am supposed to be, what I am supposed to like. Each month when my mother's subscription to *McCall's* magazine arrives I beg her for the page with the cut-out Betsy McCall doll and doll clothes. Betsy is, of course, white. But then so were all the women in the pages of *McCall's, Ladies' Home Journal, Redbook,* and the other "general interest" magazines my mother read. Housewives poised in neatly pressed shirtwaist dresses with slender belts, caught in the act of vacuuming with an Electrolux, loading laundry into a Maytag washing machine, whipping up a Betty Crocker cake, mixing their conquering husband a drink of Johnnie Walker Red. They were all white, and so were their daughters.

The flesh-colored crayon in the giant box of Crayola crayons is certainly not the color of my flesh, nor are the flesh-colored Band-Aids manufactured by Johnson & Johnson. Even the peaches and cream complexion promised in the sales pitch for Ivory soap, "99% pure," is not for me. The children in *Hi-Lites* magazines were always white, as were the human superheroes in the comic books. I think the major reason me, my brothers, and most of the black kids we knew were into Green Lantern or Spiderman as opposed to Superman or Supergirl was because we could more closely identify with and aspire to become them than their white counterparts. In westerns I was always the Indian, never the cowboy. In Tarzan movies I identified with the Africans or the apes, not Tarzan. I wanted to be Sheena, Queen of the Jungle not because she was white but because she was female and pretty, one of the only women on television who existed independently of men.

I used to watch "Father Knows Best" and "Leave It to Beaver" and "The Donna Reed Show" and "Ozzie and Harriet" and "The Patty Duke Show," but never thought of them as real, or role models, or people to emulate. I couldn't figure out how television mothers always looked perfect and never yelled, or how it was TV daddies never seemed to work but their families were still able to live well. My harried mother yelled at us regularly and my father was always busy working, and hardly ever home. Most of the women on television were uninteresting, whether the wife/mother types on the family situation comedies, or low-level career girls like Marlo Thomas as "That Girl!" or Mary Tyler Moore as an overexploited associate producer. The women I was drawn to were the ones who, if they did exist in the real world were few and far between, or were total fantasy women. Emma Peel from "The Avengers," the private detective "Honey West," Jeannie who popped out of a bottle to conjure and control on "I Dream of Jeannie," or Samantha on "Bewitched," who could do magic with a twitch of her nose. Actually, I was most enamored of Endora, Samantha's bitchy, super-powered mother, who was opinionated, obstinate, and imposed her will as she saw fit. But these women were not real. By 1968, when Diahann Carroll became the first black woman to star in her own situation comedy, "Julia," playing a nurse and single mother widowed by her husband's patriotic service in Vietnam, I no longer looked to television for reflection and inspiration. At sixteen, it was becoming clear to me that in a country that sponsored the assassination of Martin Luther King, Jr., the escalation of the war in Vietnam, the election of Richard M. Nixon, and the murder in Chicago of Black Panther Fred Hampton, the value to my life of seeing a pretty black woman on television was negligible.

The one area where black women existed in significant numbers was as entertainers, but even as a girl I knew these women were, because of their talent, exceptions, they did not serve as reflections or role models. Living in my parents' house I learned early from the sadness in their beautiful music or the overheard conversations of adults that the lives of musicians, particularly women, were harsh. Heard the stories of Bessie Smith, Billie Holiday, and Dinah Washington. Even here, black women were most often disembodied voices crackling out of a record player or radio, without visual representation. Whatever glimpse I got of these women was usually limited to a head shot on the cover of one of my parents' albums. My introduction to Gloria Lynn, Sarah Vaughan, Dinah, and Billie was as voices, faces, and feelings, not complete women.

For many years I lived what I realize now was a sheltered and charmed life as a daughter of the black middle class. I knew, liked, and did not fear white people, there was no point. I went to private schools where my classmates were the children of liberal, and sometimes left, Jews, people who, like my parents, consciously chose to educate their children in a progressive, multiracial environment. They lived in a parallel universe of their own. Separate, and if not exactly equal, certainly no better. I did not question my absence from their world any more than I longed for their presence in mine. It was a comfortable separation, at least until I entered young womanhood and realized that the black world could not employ, feed, or sustain me, before I knew what being black, female, and in the minority meant in America.

It was not until I was twelve or thirteen, moving into young womanhood, with a nascent desire for sexual and physical identity and value, that I was forced to face up to my own invisibility as a black girl. I began to realize that more often than not my physical being—brown body, heavy thighs, uncontrollable hair—wasn't seen.

As a child I read *Cinderella*, *Sleeping Beauty*, *Snow White and the Seven Dwarfs*, *Rapunzel*, in which the heroines are always white, always get the prince, live happily ever after, and always, always have long hair. In fact, if Rapunzel hadn't had that long straight hair to let down, the prince wouldn't have had anything to climb up to her tower on, would never have gotten to her. If I thought as a child these were just fairy tales and not reflections of reality, when I read *The Gift of the Magi* in junior high school English, where the man sells his prized watch to buy a comb for his wife's long, glorious hair, and she simultaneously cuts off her hair—the ultimate sacrifice for love—and sells it to buy him a watch chain, I learn that the importance of long, straight hair is not limited to stories. By adolescence, I know the importance of hair, that it is a point of entry, an attribute that women need to be considered attractive in this culture. As a black girl I learned early on that thick, kinky hair is without value, since rarely are even white women—the embodiment of beauty in a racist culture—with short hair presented as desirable. Hair, and lots of it, is required both for beauty and visibility. It is the beginning of what for most women is a lifelong obsession.

My brother Stanley and I sit on the stoop of the building we live in on 148th Street, before my father's financial success enables us to move downtown, to a better neighborhood, away from black people, which in American culture is up in status. We are hunched over, tightening our roller skates with one of those fat, silver skate keys we used back in the days before Rollerblades. I am nine, my brother is ten. He is chocolate-colored, round-faced, with thick, kinky hair cut close to the scalp in the style of the day for little black boys, teasingly called a "baldie bean." I am caramel-colored. Except for the difference in our complexions and the texture of our hair, we could pass for twins. My hair is parted in the center and hangs in two braids to the middle of my back. Its texture, closer to the straightness of white people's hair than to the tightly curled hair of black folks, is what black people too often call "good" or "pretty" hair. I learn this from adults, friends of my parents who come to visit and meeting me stroke my hair reverentially, an accident of birth or consequence of plantation rape that sets me apart from my sister and two brothers. Even as I enjoy being fawned over, I am made uncomfortable.

Two women walk past, glance our way. They are probably in their early twenties. "Ohhh, look at those long braids," one of the women says.

"Yeah. That girl gotta head of hair."

"She got that pretty hair, too," the woman says. She stops and stands looking down at my brother and me. "Can I touch it?"

I look up at her and for a moment do not know what to say. I want to ask why and then refuse, but I am afraid to, not only because I have been taught to respect adults. I am afraid that to deny this woman's small request will set me apart, make her angry, make her think that I am high siddity, fancy myself better than she.

"Can I touch it, baby?" Her voice is friendly, pleading, demanding, all at once. I nod.

She places both hands on my hairline, her fingertips in the part. She slowly, slowly, runs her hands across the crown, down to where the braids begin. Her fingers wrap my braids within tight fists and continue past the rubber bands, an inch farther to the ends. Her fists hold only air. As long as I live I will never forget the sensations evoked as this grown-up stranger caressed my hair. I feel simultaneously flattered and embarrassed, complimented and angry, all-powerful and profoundly powerless. "Thank you, baby," she says, continues up the hill. Unsure what she is thanking me for, I am unable to say, "You're welcome." I don't say anything. Instead, I bend my head down to the task at hand, furiously twist my skate key. One of my braids falls over my shoulder, swings in front me. Angrily, I flip it aside. Already finished, Stanley stands up, skates off, disappears around the corner. I hurry to catch up with him.

By the time I am fifteen, in 1967, we no longer live in Harlem, nor do I wear two braids. Four years earlier, when I was eleven, my father's successful dental practice allows him to move us from Harlem to the Upper West Side, to a building in which we are the only black family. My hair is shoulder-length now, and I try to wear it in a flip, straight to the collarbone and then ends turned up, kind of like the rich and beautiful Veronica Lodge in the "Archie" comics, although this is not easy. I want to be the Breck Girl from the television and magazine ads, every strand of shining hair always in place. It doesn't work. My hair inevitably balloons.

It is a sunny afternoon in 1967, I am walking across 125th Street toward Broadway and the bus downtown, when a voice calls, "Hey! You! With the big legs!" I look around, but can't tell where the voice is coming from, who it belongs to, or who it's talking to. The street is crowded with all sizes of women's legs in motion. "Hey! School-girl, I'm talking to you," the voice yells. That narrows it down. There are only a few girls carrying books, shouldering book bags, or wearing those telltale plaid school uniforms which, even with the skirt hiked up and lipstick smeared on, still scream "Catholic school-girl!" I try to look around surreptitiously for the voice, find that it emanates from a group of black construction workers lolling around a building site. One of the men catches my eye, grins.

"Yeah, you, girl. Where'd you get those big legs?" he says, his voice an impossible combination of a drawl and yell. I am embar-rassed and flattered. Feel violated, vulnerable, and seduced, a com-bination of emotions I will experience often and become familiar with over a lifetime interacting with men. I speed up my pace. Just past, I hear him call, "Hey, you, fine thing in the red dress!" I look down just to double-check, but I am not wearing a red dress. Now that I'm out of his line of vision, he is no longer talking to me, has moved on to the next female. I am both disappointed and relieved.

Fifteen years old, I am obsessed with the cosmic questions of young womanhood: Who am I? How do I look? Is my hair okay? Will anyone ever love me? Am I pretty? Even though I have not started dating, have barely been past second base, have no real understanding of what sexuality is, I can feel its presence, know that it is crucially important, to me and to others. Internally, it appears suddenly in spurts, then vanishes. I am at moments physically hypersensitive, aware each time thigh brushes thigh, a swinging arm touches the side of a breast, of the weight between my legs that throbs and subsides. The eyes of men, passing carelessly over me, leave hot trails on my skin. They confirm the external world's awareness of my sex. Feeling them, my body shifts, squirms, realigns itself, simultaneously preens and contracts. I hurry home, "Big legs, big legs, big legs" resounding in my ears.

When I am a teenager and blossoming into a full-breasted, big-legged, round-hipped young black woman, the prevalent symbols of youthful beauty were models. First among them was a skinny-legged, flat-chested, knock-kneed blonde model from England named Twiggy.

Twiggy was to me and my friends, black and white, what Kate Moss is to many teenagers in the 1990s, the dominant image of feminine beauty. It does not occur to me at the time that there is anything at all wrong with Twiggy; all inadequacies are mine. She is not too thin, I am too fat. She does not look awkward, I am the one who is clumsy and out of place. Her breasts are not too small, mine are too big. Even though neither I or any of my friends even faintly resemble Twiggy, we see her image over and over in *Seventeen* and other magazines and with repetition she becomes our ideal. We diet, draw pale half-moons under our eyes with wrinkle erasing sticks in search of her startled, deer-caught-in-the-car-headlights look, mimic her style of dress, call one another "Luv." But the power Twiggy possesses derives not simply from her being the current embodiment of beauty, she is also a female cultural icon, arriving at the height of America's fascination with all things British. She is a total package. We want to not only look like Twiggy but be her. We want her life. Along with the Beatles, the Rolling Stones, and Carnaby Street, Twiggy is the latest fab import from England, the ultimate source of mid-1960s white pop culture, the feminine representation of the British invasion. The notion that all you have to do to be famous, rich, and beloved is to be a Twiggy clone does not seem either unreasonable or unreal when I am fifteen.

When I enter the house that day from 125th Street my mother says, "Is everything all right, Jill?"

"I'm fat, I'm ugly, I'll never be skinny," I wail.

"Skinny? Why would you want to be skinny?" My mother, five foot three and a hundred and sixteen pounds, hands me a tissue, exhales smoke. I sob harder. How can I expect my mother to understand?

"I don't want to be big this, big that! I want to be skinny, beautiful, famous, have everyone love me." My mother gives one of those patient here-we-go sighs.

"What brought all this on?" she asks. I tell her about my walk, how nice it was until the man called out to "Big Legs" and I realized he was making fun of me.

"I'm fat, I'm ugly, my legs are too big!" A fresh cascade of tears runs down my cheeks. What does Mommy do? Does she gather me in her arms, soothe me, assure me that I am perfect just the way I am? But no. Instead, she laughs. I sob louder.

"It's a compliment," she says through laughter. "Big legs, that's a compliment. Men like those big, pretty legs like you and your Aunt Florence have."

My father's sister, Aunt Florence, unlike most adults, listens more than she talks. She is not petite and slim like my sister and mother, but tall and "healthy" like me. In 1994, my Aunt Florence gets very sick and has both legs amputated above the knee. She tells me that I now have the pretty legs for both of us and not to waste them. When I go to visit I wear a dress or skirt, sit with our legs crossed. Recently, her voice filled with wonder, she tells me of waking up mornings with her legs aching after dreaming of dancing all night, her feet hurt too, taking Tylenol and waiting for it to work its magic on those big, pretty legs.

"What about you, your legs?" I ask. My mother shifts her weight, extends one of her legs. The muscle in the back of her calf bulges. My mother has always worn high heels on her tiny feet.

"I've got good legs, but I always wished they were bigger," she says thoughtfully.

"Really?" It is the first time it has occurred to me that except for breasts, anything on a woman's body should be bigger. Sad to say, this is a revolutionary thought.

"Really. You've got big, pretty legs, you should know that. Forget those white girls with those skinny giraffe legs. Next time you see your Aunt Florence, look at her legs. Yours are just like them, you should be proud of them. That man was just paying you a compliment." I wrap my mind around this statement and am soothed until my mother adds, "But it's low life for men to yell—even compliments—at you on the street. Whatever you do, never respond."

At fifteen, hurtling toward womanhood, in the end I am left more confused than before, unsettled by the sense of ugliness, violation, and thrill that the man's attention and compliment—once explained by my mother—made me feel, made uncertain by the knowledge of both my physical vulnerability and my need for bodily affirmation. I am embarrassed and frightened that in a world of little confirmation and much negation a few shouted words from a man, "low life" or otherwise, could make me, in such a short space of time, feel both ugly and beautiful, visible and invisible, frightened and seduced.

My mother is light brown, my father very dark. I do not think much about this when I am young except when they remind the four of us kids that to intelligent, good people skin color is an inappropriate basis on which to judge others. What was important was who you were, what you thought, the deeds you did. "Beauty is as beauty does" was an oft-repeated adage in our household, words I grew to accept as true. Still, outside the universe my parents created I could not help but notice that most of the beautiful women were white, and the few black women white people gave their props and admitted were gorgeous were usually very light-skinned, like Lena Horne. Even in the black community, ninety-nine times out of a hundred if a black woman was described as beautiful you could bet your bottom dollar she was light-skinned. Attractiveness seemed to increase as levels of melanin decreased. There's an old rhyme that goes, "If you're light, you're all right, if you're black, get back, if you're yellow, you're mellow." I don't recall when I first heard it, but I was very young. I knew, according to the laws of my family, it was wrong to judge others by or to trade upon one's own skin color, but it was also clear to me that doing so had currency in both black and white communities.

Back in 1963, at age eleven, I call my dark-skinned best friend Lynn "black." It was not a compliment. In the early 1960s black had about the same negative connotations as "nigger." I said it in the midst of an argument between a group of girls over who was most beautiful; whoever was would have the starring role in the game we were about to play. It was summer and we were standing on Pennacook Street on Martha's Vineyard, a block from the beach. Lynn, copping a plea for herself as vocally as the rest of us, said, "I'm prettiest," and I looked her dead in the eye and said, "You're black." I spoke these words with arrogance, incredulity, and cruelty, the tone of my voice as much as my words communicated the cultural conditioning that eleven years of parental lectures had been unable to erase, that to be both prettiest and black was impossible. I cannot remember what Lynn said, if anything. I do remember the stricken look in her eyes. I knew at that moment I'd said something terrible, stepped over an important line, one that I did not know until that moment was there. I do remember that when we went home that evening, neither one of us felt prettiest.

As a girl and young woman, hair, body, and color were society's trinity in determining female beauty and identity, the cultural and value-laden gang of three that formed the boundaries and determined the extent of women's visibility, influence, and importance. For the most part, they still are. We learn as girls that in ways both subtle and obvious, personal and political, our value as females is largely determined by how we look. As we enter womanhood, the pervasive power of this trinity is demonstrated again and again in how we are treated by the men we meet, the men we work for, the men who wield power, how we treat each other and, most of all, ourselves. For black women, the domination of physical aspects of beauty in women's definition and value render us invisible, partially erased, or obsessed, sometimes for a lifetime, since most of us lack the major talismans of Western beauty. Black women find themselves involved in a lifelong effort to self-define in a culture that provides them no positive reflection.

By the time I turned eighteen and graduated from high school in 1970, I was obsessed with trying to figure out exactly what it meant to be a young person, a woman, a black person, and particularly a black woman, in a time of tremendous political, cultural, and social turmoil, much of which consigned women to the traditional role of unseen helpmate, bodies at the rally, or sexual vessel, or excluded us altogether. I knew that the few roles the culture offered to women—wife, mother, secretary, sex object—were unacceptable, but what were the alternatives? Then along came Angela Yvonne Davis.

Angela Davis was the first black woman who was alive, only a few years older than me, who seemed to embody many of the elements of who I wanted to be in one body. She was smart, beautiful, political, outspoken, talented, self-defined, single, and famous. She burst into the public consciousness after being accused of supplying the guns used in a courtroom shoot-out by members of the Black Panther Party in San Rafael, California, in which four people were killed. This alleged act put her on the FBI's Ten Most Wanted list. She was tried and eventually acquitted of all charges. Thirty years later, ignoring her subsequent work as a writer and teacher, the culture has attempted to reduce Davis' importance to the sum of her enormous Afro. But as an eighteen-year-old black woman, Davis meant far more to me and my peers. That she may well have had the most perfect, bushy, symmetrical natural I've ever seen was affirming, but incidental. Style may have reflected substance, it did not determine it. It may have been Davis' hair that first caught my eye, but it was her courage, intellect, and commitment to what she believed in that touched not only my spirit, but the spirits of many people, particularly young black women. Here was a black woman who not only looked different, but behaved differently. A sister who was visible and vocal whose beliefs and actions profoundly irked and challenged the status quo. For many black women who came of age in the 1950s and 60s feeling unattractive and inadequate, knowing that even if we wanted to we could never be Barbie, Davis represented the possibility of a more realistic and compelling identity.

A child of Birmingham's black middle class, a member of the Communist Party fired from UCLA for her party membership, a woman who had known the four Sunday school girls blown up by segregationists in the basement of Birmingham's 16th Street Baptist Church in 1963, Davis touched me deeply. An uncomfortable, rebellious, and political child of the black middle class, I immediately connected with Davis and in her saw some reflection of who I was and would like to be. She suggested who I might become: a visible, outspoken, political woman. In the eyes of many Americans, the privileged good girl in blackface gone bad.

In Angela Davis, the biographies I read as a girl, tales of Harriet Tubman, Sojourner Truth, Phyllis Wheatley, Ida B. Wells, ordinary black women whom circumstances made extraordinary, came to life. I wore a "Free Angela" button, handed out leaflets, attended rallies of support. I devoured everything I could find written by or about her, wanting to know what a Communist really was, how revolution worked. I went and bought Karl Marx' *Das Kapital* and Franz Fanon's *The Wretched of the Earth.* Angela Davis was the first living black woman who suggested to me that the struggle for a broader definition of what it could mean to be a woman in America, for self-definition, was not merely a physical but a political struggle, and that it would be ongoing.

Nearly three decades after I turned eighteen in 1970, the issues that I struggled with as a girl and young woman coming of age still dominate, the trinity of hair, body, and complexion prevail. It is only their manifestations that have changed.

In a wonderful collection of essays called *Home,* published in

1966, Leroi Jones, now Amiri Baraka, commented about television that the best thing about it was that black people weren't on it. Nowadays, our faces are all over television. Most of the time we're being arrested, robbing, shooting, posturing on talk shows, writhing in music videos. Black women are most often seen in music videos, gyrating in sexually explicit pantomime, the close-up, more often than not, on our jiggling butts, breasts, or open thighs, although you may see a yard or two of synthetic hair fly by now and then. I may have known the women on my parents' album covers only as singing heads without bodies, but at least I knew they had heads. What I know after an afternoon watching music videos is that black women's bodies can now be used to sell things too. What's in their heads is irrelevant. Sometimes I think that, overall, invisibility might have been better.

Aside from a brief period in the late 1950s and 60s when the "Afro" was in style, the natural texture of most black women's hair remains, as it has historically been, unacceptable. The apparently neverending popularity of a variety of straightening devices, from the hot comb to chemical straighteners—now euphemistically called "relaxers," as if the problem is that sister's hair is uptight and all we need to do is to get it to cool out—attests to this. The proliferation in the last decade of hair weaves and braided extensions is a manifestation of black women's desire for hair that is not only straight but long, the better to toss. To black women, the message sent by the culture of beauty remains the same, i.e., that we genetically lack a fundamental element of desirability. The difference is that now we have thousands of products marketed specifically to us, the vast majority of them produced by white companies. This has nothing to do with inclusion and everything to do with cash. Just as when I was growing up we all knew the answer to the refrain of the Clairol ads, "Is it true blondes have more fun?," today when the actress Cybill Shepherd, blonde, straight-haired, and hawking L'Oreal hair products, declares she uses them "Because I'm worth it," we all know the flip side is that those of us who don't are worth less.

Not much has changed. The infrequent times when black women are portrayed as objects of desire in popular culture, their hair is invariably long, their features usually more Caucasian than Negroid, their bodies, since most often they are models, skinny. Happy as I was to see the images of black models Naomi Sims, Pat Cleveland, Alva Chin, Iman, and Pat Johnson break onto the scene when I was a young woman, it was clear most black women did not—and could not—look like them with their narrow noses, high cheekbones, and long, silky manes. Thirty years later, the same can be said of Veronica Webb and Tyra Banks. Even the popularity of the dark-skinned, British-born Naomi Campbell, whose natural hair is often shrouded in wigs, represents merely an updated version of white beauty in blackface, but this time with a twist: the black woman as exotic, animalistic, sexualized dominatrix. Still, note Campbell's long hair and colored contact lenses, making it clear that she is not the loathed and dreaded authentic black woman.

Stephanie Berry is a brown-skinned woman in her early forties who has been acting for thirteen years, and has recently begun getting television roles. Berry looks more like Every Sister than a model. "I have never been the love interest," she says. "I am always a single mother. I am always the parent of a male black child and he is always a victim or perpetrator of violence. I usually don't have a husband, and if I do, he dies too. I am always grieving." Berry tells the story of a recent audition. "I knew I was a grieving mother. I walked in and said, 'Okay, what happened to my baby this time? What did my boy do?' I was trying to make light. They didn't find it funny. I did not get the part."

In the last thirty years there has been little real alteration of the beauty industry's marketing of whiteness as the norm, the standard to which all the rest of us should aspire. For black girls and women this journey is as psychically devastating as it is omnipresent. Even if we manage to get rid of our hips, breasts, waistlines, grow our hair, get a weave or extensions, even if we go blonde, we will never possess the fundamental ingredient for female beauty in America, and that is whiteness.

In this climate, we conveniently forget that for most black Americans light skin is the result of rape and sexual exploitation during slavery; we are only interested in the proffered rewards or favor we believe come with lighter skin color. It is a psychological given that all people feel most immediately comfortable with those who look like them. It is not coincidence that the primary image of African American women we see in popular culture, particularly television and print advertisements, are light-skinned. It's gotten to the point that I often have to see a commercial two or three times to figure out if the green-eyed, crinkly-haired woman selling cereal or soda is black. If she's dark-skinned, chances are she's selling something that's a drag to use, like toilet bowl cleanser or a laxative. What we are witnessing is the rise of the biracial as favored black woman, even though it's stretching the point to suggest any of us are preferred. At the millennium, the culture has taken their contempt and our erasure one step further. Two of the most visible and acceptable images of black women in the eyes of the dominant culture are those offered by RuPaul and, occasionally, the Chicago Bulls' Dennis Rodman, black men in drag.

Black Americans twist the fruit of our enslavement into a prized possession. As much as black people don't like to talk about or admit it, a color caste system remains a dominant aspect of our communities, particularly for women. Put a truly beautiful chocolate-colored woman side by side with an average-looking beige one and

I guarantee you that most black people will declare the lighter-skinned one prettier. Look at black couples and notice how often the woman's complexion is lighter than the man's, evidence that we continue, consciously or not, to find light-skinned women, and the increased chance that they will produce lighter-skinned children, more valuable. This is our version of "marrying up." Listen even to the language we use when talking about color. Light-skinned people are described as "fair"; language as value judgment. People are often described as "dark, *but* beautiful," as if their complexion were something to overcome. Too often, we hold darker children to behavioral standards that lighter children are not required to meet, as if their complexion confers upon them a state of grace that excuses or mitigates misbehavior, instant entitlement based upon color that extends, especially for women, into adulthood. In describing newborns, what black people always tell you is about the baby's color and the texture of their hair, even when they cannot recall the infant's name. We have a plethora of myths and folk wisdom relating to hair and complexion: A bald head on a baby means the child will have "good" hair, a thick head of hair means naps will follow, an infant's adult complexion can be judged by the color of the palms of its hands or soles of its feet, a clothespin on the nose will keep it from spreading, becoming a wide, Negroid nose.

Flip through an issue of *Vogue, Elle, Mademoiselle,* or any other women's magazine (a misnomer, since they should more accurately be called men's magazines, since their focus is on how men want to configure women), and black women are largely absent. When we are present, it is as images that conform to white notions of black beauty. There is no doubt that some of these women are beautiful, but Naomi Campbell is not most of us, any more than Kate Moss is most white women. The difference is that above and beyond the destructive myths of beauty, white women have a whole white culture that confers on them, in whatever twisted ways, the myriad rewards of whiteness. She is at least viewed as a woman, in the sweepstakes, and visible.

Most women, white and black, are not comforted by the dominant myths of beauty. The difference for black women is that we do not feel simply ugly, but totally outside, irrelevant, invisible. The significant and continuing success of *Essence,* the only fashion and beauty magazine targeted toward black women, is due in large part to the visibility it gives to black women in all our diversity of color, hair, and body. Almost three decades after its debut in 1970, *Essence* remains the only magazine that consistently recognizes and embraces the true range of black beauty. In the pages of *Essence,* our beauty is not dependent on our degree of whiteness or the subtle and overt racist and sexist fantasies of male photographers and art directors of black women as exotic, animalistic, overly sexualized objects of domination, degradation, and desire. In these pages, black women's beauty is normal, not aberrant. As a black woman, I have been trying to figure out what is beautiful, and functional, and comfortable for me and my sisters for most of my life.

Over the last ten years I've been having my hair cut shorter and shorter. In the late summer of 1996, when I am forty-four, I have my hair shaved to the scalp with an electric razor. When I leave my head is covered with a faint memory of brown and silver peach fuzz, I am as close to bald as I can get without lathering up and using a straight razor. I do this because I am tired of everything about hair—having it, combing it, thinking about it, plain feeling it. So, to test my theory that for me hair has finally become obsolete, I got rid of it. I want to see how people react to me, and how I react to myself, hairless. After the first few days, when I wake up startled by my own reflection in the mirror, I come to love it. I like the way it looks, the way it feels bristly when I run my hand over it from any direction, the fact that after four decades I have achieved hair that requires no maintenance.

The response of others is profound. Most black men's eyes skip over me rapidly, distastefully, as if they do not care to see someone who looks like me. I catch pure disdain in the eyes of several. A few stare, look intrigued, and rap to me, although most of these are young enough to be my children. Black women in general—with the exception of the few who are also either bald or wearing short naturals or dreadlocks, who give me a solidarity smile or compliment me—look at me as if I am totally unattractive, insane, and vaguely threatening. It is as if in deciding to be bald I am challenging our collective obsession with hair. Maybe I am. White people, women and men, look surprised and stare at me as I go by. Many people, across race, particularly women, give me a sympathetic smile, assuming, perhaps, that I am a cancer patient undergoing chemotherapy. Whatever a specific individual's response, the most interesting thing about being bald is that I am no longer invisible. Like it or not, everyone sees me. It is a wonderful sensation. Maybe a giant step in black women gaining visibility would be if we all shaved our heads. We would be both immediately visible and connected.

Barring such drastic action, a possible first step would be in acknowledging the commonality of our experiences as black girls and women in a hostile and alien culture. Sometimes that affirmation comes from simply making eye contact. Or talking to girls about self-image. Or teaching young women how to look at popular culture critically. Or telling another woman that she looks nice. That is sisterhood.

Several days after I cut my hair I walk to the subway station. The woman rapidly climbing the steps ahead of me has dark brown skin, a slim frame. I cannot see how old she is. A teenage girl walks slightly behind her. One of the girl's hands casually touches the woman's dreadlocks as she talks. As I close the distance between us I hear the girl say, "Really, Mom, you could go to the hairdresser and they twist them up right, fix up your locks, they'd look nice. People would notice you, people would be looking from across the street."

The woman turns slightly to look back at her daughter. She is smiling. "Forget it. This ain't no hairstyle," she says as I pull alongside her. She is probably in her early thirties. I reach out my hand and we slap five, briefly clasp hands, laugh. It is a moment of unspoken understanding, communion, knowing that hair, and so much of what we thought mattered to the business of our being women, doesn't matter at all, or much, or certainly not enough for her to go to a beauty salon and have her low-maintenance dreadlocks styled. It is obsolete. That there is too much work to be done and that she with her non–salon selected locks and me with my damn near bald head, and all the other sisters struggling for loving self-definition, are bad as we wanna be. At the bottom of the steps her daughter peels off, heading downtown. We climb the last flight of steps in tandem, going in the same direction.

THE DAWNING OF THE PATRIARCH

WHEN I WAS FOURTEEN my father came home and tried to throw the Christmas tree out the window of our eleventh-floor apartment. To this day, I don't know why. He was Daddy, the boss, and pretty much did what he wanted, without explanation.

We always got our tree on Christmas Eve. Well, not "we," exactly. The menfolk went out and bought the tree, the womenfolk stayed home baking goodies. I accepted this as part of the glorious Nelson tradition that demanded that we not only have the best, but be the best, that there was a preferred way of doing everything, and that way was however my father wanted it. Going to Martha's Vineyard in the summer, beginning in 1956 before the island got famous and crowded with the nouveau riche, or for rides in my father's imported French Citroen on Sunday afternoons, usually when the weather was too rainy or cold for him to abandon us and go to the golf course, were also parts of that tradition. It was defined by being first and having the best as my father, breadwinner and patriarch, defined it. It was the way he did things, and the way he did things was right and good.

It wasn't until I was a grown woman, my parents long divorced, that my mother revealed to me the roots of that glorious Nelson Christmas tree tradition.

"I wish your brothers would go ahead and get the damn tree," she says. It is the week before Christmas.

"We always get the tree on Christmas Eve."

"Well, I'd just as soon get the sucker in here, up, and decorated. I'm tired of waiting till the last minute."

"But we always get it Christmas Eve. It's so exciting that way. It's a tradition."

"A tradition?" My mother gives one of those guttural, from the chest "Hah!" laughs, almost a snicker, but fuller.

"That's when Daddy and the boys always got it when we were kids."

"I know. But that was because your father was cheap, didn't want to pay all that money for a dead tree. He'd wait until Christmas Eve because the prices went down. Christmas trees aren't worth anything on Christmas."

"Really?" I am mildly stunned. "Are you just saying that?" I ask hopefully.

"No, I'm not just saying that," my mother snaps. "You kids just want to romanticize everything 'Dad' did, well, 'Dad' did a lot of crazy things too . . ." She keeps talking, bursting my childhood bubble, telling me about other rituals of my father's whose basis is not in tradition or well-thought-out life choices but in his own psyche and cold, hard pragmatism. I half listen, internally wean myself from the false holiday tradition and defend against my mother's words.

The thing about having angrily divorced parents is that when one speaks about the other you lose a part of your past in exchange for the truth, because neither has any investment in fronting for the other anymore.

"God, I can't believe it," I say.

"Well, believe it. Why do you think it always took them so long to get back with the tree? Because by Christmas Eve most of the healthy big ones were sold, and Dad had to find the biggest, most perfect tree for the least money."

Later, on the telephone, I ask my favorite Aunt Florence, my father's sister, nicknamed "Butter" because when she smiles her cheeks bunch up like pats, about their childhood.

"When you were little, Florence, did you all have a Christmas tree?"

"Yes . . ."

"When did you get it?"

"Christmastime." Something in Florence's voice suggests this is a very stupid question. I laugh.

"I mean, what day?"

"Right before . . . I think Christmas Eve . . ." I can almost hear her mind rummaging through seventy-five years of memories.

"So it was a tradition!" I say. I cannot wait to tell my mother the next time I see her that Daddy wasn't cheap, he was traditional. Ha! On second thought, maybe I'll keep it to myself. Why stir up trouble?

"Well, I guess you could say that." She chuckles.

"You know, Butter. Getting the tree the same day every year. Who went, your father and brothers?"

"Now wait a minute, let me think . . ." Florence hums. "Come to think of it, and it was a long time ago, I don't think we got our tree Christmas Eve . . ." She's quiet, the only sound the rustling of the past. I knew I should have hung up after I received the answer I wanted. Florence's memory pops into place.

"That's right. We didn't buy a tree, you didn't buy trees back then, we were too poor." Her words rush out, ancient history finding voice. "That's right. A cousin would bring a tree from the country a few days before Christmas. We never bought one."

"Didn't Dad, Ralph, Babe, and Granddaddy ever go?"

Ralph and Howard, Jr., nicknamed Babe, are my father's brothers.

"They might have, but not on Christmas Eve. Your grandmother wouldn't have stood for all that foolishness. For true, for true," Florence singsongs.

"Thanks," I say sadly.

"Whatever you need, honey. See you soon."

So okay, okay, my mother is right again.

Until I am eleven we live in Harlem, on 148th Street. My father's dental office is on Central Park South, eighty-nine blocks downtown. My father keeps an apartment on 57th Street, where he lives during the week. On the weekdays, it is us and our mother. We do homework, talk, listen to records, watch television, argue, read, play board games. Alone, my mother cooks, cleans, talks to us, reads, and smokes Viceroy cigarettes, happily. My father, an ex-smoker, is not there to harass her or be jealous of the attention she gives not to him, but to words. On Friday, after school, we start cleaning up the house, getting our act together. Daddy's coming home.

Only much later do I realize that this feature of our lives—as totally accepted as our "tradition" with the tree—is far from the average family's norm, black or white. It isn't until we're women that my sister says, "When we were kids I thought everyone's father went to work on Monday and didn't come home until the week-end. When I'd go to my friend's house after school and her father would come home for dinner, I thought it was because he didn't have a job." In college I read about South African mine workers and they remind me of Daddy, the way they leave their wives and families, not seeing them for months while they went underground to drill for diamonds. Of course, my father was in America, above ground, drilling teeth, only gone for five days, and left us voluntarily, so maybe the only connection is how happy we feel when he comes home. It is as if only then are we complete, the family made whole by my father's arrival. Like the Christmas tree "tradition," for much of my life this seems appropriate, normal, the way it was and therefore the way it should be. My mother, his sons, his daughters defer to my father. He rules when both absent and present. When he is not present, we imagine what he would want us to do, how he would require that something be done, and do it his way. It is not until I am a woman that I begin to think about and try to understand that life with Daddy was my introduction to living under patriarchy. As a girl, it does not occur to me that there is a complex social structure that props up my father's authority, nor that he would need it. I only know what is: that my father's word is law, that even my mother of the sharp tongue and wry wit does not argue or disagree with him very often, that as children we would be wise to obey and keep our mouths shut. I also know that it is my brothers who feel my father's wrath most powerfully, even when all of us commit the same transgression. In this way I learn that what boys do is usually, somehow, more important. Living in my father's house I am relieved by this because it allows me to escape his anger and disappointment. It is not until I am grown and gone that I begin to recognize the price I paid, that girls so often pay, for being deemed less important in the patriarchal scheme of things, in Daddy's world, where he who has all the power giveth and taketh away.

It has taken me most of my adult life to even begin to understand who my father was when I was a girl growing up, and to accept and reconcile the way he was then with the way he is now. To separate the way I see my father from the way I see men, and to swallow the bitter lesson I learned from life with my father, that even though the unspoken promise when I was growing up said it would, to give away all the power hoping to get love in return does not work. When I was a child and young woman, my father was the absolute boss, larger than life, the sun around whom everyone in our family orbited, whose rays we needed, or believed we needed, to survive. He was the breadwinner, the provider, the one who made upper-middle-class life as we knew it possible. Head of the family even in his frequent absence, the first man I ever loved and the first patriarch whose rule I lived under. It is from my father that I learn about men and to love them. It is also from him that I come to know the absolute and often mercurial rule of men, and to distrust it.

The six of us sit around the dinner table on a summer night when I am nine. The conversation is about vegetables. My baby brother Ralphie refuses to eat them, clamps his lips together so tightly they lose their fullness and disappear inward, opening them only to beg my mother for a reprieve. When my father is not home, my mother relents, makes him eat another piece of meatloaf or a potato instead, although I never understand the nutritional logic behind this substitution of food groups. When Daddy's home, Ralphie is rarely cut any slack. My father is not a man who cuts any of us much slack, my brothers least of all. Fathers have a way of devouring their sons even as they love them, in the process of trying to make men out of them not allowing them to be boys, and my father is no stranger to this. They simultaneously urge their sons to surpass them and threaten them with abandonment and punishment if they do. My father focuses most of this crazy, destabilizing, good cop, bad cop energy on his oldest son and namesake, my big brother Stanley. While my sister and I are unavoidably swept up in the We Are Nelsons theme that dominates the text and subtext of our family's life, we are not privy to the dickpolitik of that message, that doo wop chorus of Greeks in blackface—my father pledged Kappa at Howard University, the most prestigious fraternity, and even had the letter K branded on his chest to prove it—chanting "Be a man! Be a man! Be a Man!"

Other than on weekends, my father was usually absent. The few and far between times that I spent alone with my father were glorious. I was the girl-woman of my father's dreams: young, adoring, non-threatening, without back talk. Like the hundred pounds of clay from the Gene Chandler song, my father molded me in his image. My father took me to the Plaza Hotel's Oak Bar and other places and taught me the difference between wine, hard liquor, and champagne. Sometimes we went window shopping along Fifth Avenue, my father pointing out to me how to recognize not only what was beautiful, appealing to the eye, but also what was well made, sturdy, what would last. Over and over, my father would tell the story of coming into my room early in the morning when I was a baby and how I'd be standing up in my crib, just grinning and laughing, as if I'd been waiting for him. "You always loved me so," he'd say, grinning too. "Even when you were a tiny baby." And my father loved me back. He was the one who spoiled me when he did drop in. It was my mother, omnipresent, who taught me the real deal and forced me to be practical.

At those times when we were alone together I was Daddy's girl, and loved every minute of it. Because I was not his son I was not expected to grow into a proud representative of my father's notion of manhood, to reflect, mirror, yet never threaten my father's male ego. My father gave to me, and I took what he gave, without animosity or reservation. It is not until I am an adult that I understand my father could afford to adore me because my gender made me non-threatening. And because I was his daughter, none of the complications of sexuality affected our relationship. He always made me feel that I was a wonderful person. My appeal was not dependent upon my sexuality. He set a standard that is still with me today, a sense of my entitlement to both the attention and respect of men independent of my genitalia, not an easy standard to achieve. I have found, more often than not, that men have a difficult time both adoring and respecting women.

When my father is home, meals are determined by his possible mood. They are tense affairs, my mother telepathically communicating to the four of us the same message, "Act nice, act nice, don't set your father off." Experience has taught us to hear and heed, but it didn't seem to matter how we behaved. If my father was in a good mood, the greatest faux pas passed unnoticed. If my father was in a bad mood, no amount of docile, perfect-Negro-children-of-the-perfect-Negro-man behavior made any difference.

Most nights my mother put broccoli or carrots or whatever the vegetable du jour was on Ralph's plate, perhaps hoping he'd grown to like them overnight. When he saw them, he'd look up at her, eyes pleading and beginning to tear, and before he'd even start to whine, my mother would say, "That's all right, just eat around them." But this night my father is home. When Ralphie, spying string beans, gives my mother his imploring look, she ignores him. Ralph is five or six, not old enough to have learned a cardinal rule of the family dynamic, that Silence is Golden really means, "If you don't mention something to your parents most of the time they're too busy and tired to remember it," because he declares, "I don't want any vegetables!" My mother says, in a voice somewhere between a whisper and a hiss, "All right. Just eat around them."

"No, it is not. Eat your goddamn vegetables!" my father says. I do not recall my father actually shouting, then or at other times. But when he spoke it was with such authority it often seemed as if he was yelling. My sister, Lynn, brother Stanley, and I glance quickly at each other. It's that familiar "Oh God, here we go" look. Just as quickly, we look down at our plates, into the green nothingness of string beans.

Ralphie's eyes tear up behind his glasses. "I can't. I hate them. Mommy," he wails, but no reprieve is possible. Daddy's home, Daddy's home, but not to stay.

"Eat," my father says. "Vegetables are good for you, they'll help you grow big and strong."

"Daddy, I can't, I don't like them, they make me sick," Ralphie snivels.

My father snorts contemptuously. "Don't you want to grow up to be big and strong like your brother and sisters?"

"No." Wrong move. Honesty may be the best policy in the abstract, but there is nothing abstract about Daddy.

My father shakes his head, a gesture of anger, disgust, and sadness, looks out the window across the Hudson River, to New Jersey. "I don't know about you, Ralphie. Maybe you came from New Jersey, you're from the Mix family, from across the river. I might have to send you back." He laughs. Whenever one of his children does something that does not fit into my father's notion of how we should behave, he separates himself from us, casually, jokingly—as if it is ever possible to be casual or funny about this—disavows paternity. The Mix family is my father's especially constructed purgatory for Ralphie, his youngest child. At best, when his status as the last born works to his benefit, Ralphie is the baby of the family; when it does not, he is the runt of the litter. I do not know where my father got the name "Mix" from, if he simply pulled it from the air or specifically chose it because it implies a hodgepodge, but it suggests that Ralph does not belong, is part of a mistake, a mix-up. The three of us look up from our plates at Daddy, hoping it's over. I'm ready to sell Ralphie across the river to some losers in New Jersey to keep the peace. Blue skies, looking at me, nothing but blue skies do I see.

"But you still have to eat your vegetables, even if you are a Mix," my father says. Those blue skies vanish. Stormy weather, since my dad and I are together, seems it's raining all the time.

"Eat," my mother whispers.

Sentenced to death by vegetable, Ralphie finds the smallest string bean, slits it open lengthwise, removes each seed. Tears run down his face, plop onto his plate. He spears the bean, gingerly lifts it toward his mouth, hesitates. "Eat it!" my father orders.

My mother leans across the table, pushes his milk glass closer to his hand. "Just chew it a little, drink some milk, and swallow, baby," she encourages.

"He's not a goddamn baby! If you'd stop treating him like one he'd eat all his food," my father says.

My mother retreats.

I sit there, shovel in string beans, watch Ralphie from underneath lowered lids, can feel the heat of his hot tears against my face. I chew harder, swallow. Ralphie lifts the fork to his mouth, inserts the single, bare-bones bean. He flinches when his mouth closes, face contorts, eyes look panicked. His jaw does not move.

"Chew!" my father commands.

"Have a sip of milk," my mother suggests. The three of us pause, forks in midair, mesmerized, watching Ralph. He grabs his milk, opens his mouth, takes an enormous gulp, as if he hopes the milk will be a river, wash the bean downstream, away from his taste buds, into his stomach.

"Chew it!" my father says. Ralph begins to choke, little dribbles of milk seep from the corners of his mouth.

"Chew. Don't you spit out any food at my table," my father orders. Ralph coughs harder, lips still closed.

"Stanley, he's choking," my mother pleads. My father dismisses her with a wave of his hand.

"Eat your food." My brother looks at my father and gulps. Milk suddenly flows out of his nose. He opens his mouth and out comes more milk, accompanied by coughing, choking noises. I watch the flow of liquid from my brother's nose and mouth, fascinated by its amazing grossness. I am awed by Ralphie's daring, his nerve, his commitment to his beliefs, prejudices, taste buds, whatever. I am impressed by his audacity, his willingness to take on the wrath of my father so boldly. For the first time I glimpse how strong, stubborn, opinionated—in short, what a Nelson—my seemingly quiet, frail, introspective baby brother is. It is one of the first times I remember doubting my father's judgment, his omniscience, and his authority. Can it be that he is so distracted by the beans that he does not see in Ralphie's resistance the values he so prizes, determination, obstinacy, belief in one's self? That Ralphie is no Mix imported from New Jersey, but a Nelson; you reap what you sow.

"Stop. Stop it!" my father commands. Milk flows unabated. My mother rises from her seat, stands behind Ralph's chair, patting his back with one hand to ease the coughing, mopping at his nose and mouth with the other. The flow of milk subsides. With a final cough he expels a last stream of milk, in the middle of which floats that single string bean, untouched by teeth marks. My mother rubs his back in soothing, circular motions.

"Go to your room!" my father says in disgust. I sit, staring at the pool of milk, mucus, and string beans in his abandoned plate. It dawns on me that Ralphie has won, once again hasn't eaten his vegetables. I send him a silent wave of congratulations.

"All right, the show's over. Eat your dinner!" my father says. I can tell by the tone of his voice he knows he's lost. I bend my head and eat every bean on my plate, strings, seeds, and all.

My father was not a physically violent man, although he occasionally spanked us, usually when we'd done something so heinous that my mother declined to discipline us herself, passing that dubious privilege on to Daddy. It must have been an awkward role for him to play, coming home not as the successful hunter, the hero out there fighting and conquering the forces of racism and capitalism to provide for his family, but as the enforcer. For the most part, my father's violence was not physical, but emotional. I do not believe he had any idea it was violence at all. I think he thought he was being a good father, giving us guidance, setting standards, and in some ways he was. But his personality was so dominant that it often felt violent. When he was home the air of our apartment became saturated with his tension. We lived not exactly in fear of the unknown, but on alert. My father dominated with his authoritative presence, physical stature, the coiled spring of his mercurial emotional presence. We learned to behave ourselves when he was around, to put on a happy face, to expect the unexpected.

Years after we are grown and have not lived with my father for decades, talking about our childhood my brother Stanley says, "I don't remember any fun times with Dad. I hated those stupid drives and outings he used to take us on, we were just there, he never really interacted with us, did he? I can't remember ever playing ball with him or any of those things fathers and sons are supposed to do . . . Wait. I think we played catch two times in the hallway when we lived in Harlem."

In the end it is the baby of the bunch, Ralphie, composer and lyricist, who puts it best, describes my father's visits to his family as, "Like God came home. Really great. You didn't know him that well, and then he was gone."

Each of us has been uniquely shaped by my father, and there is no small connection between my outspokenness as an adult woman and the silence I felt was often demanded to successfully navigate life with Daddy. I remember once as a girl the four of us are sitting on the porch on Martha's Vineyard with my father and he says if we did some thing or the other we'd be "healthy, wealthy, and . . .," him just letting the incomplete sentence hang there, and me murmuring "Wise." But when my father asks, "Who said that?" I cannot tell from his voice if he is angry or pleased so I say nothing, do not own up that it was me until he offers a monetary reward to whoever said "Wise," and I know that, at least in this instance, speaking up was a good thing. That this time my father will embrace and not shun me.

On weekends and especially during Christmastime my father played the music of Edward Kennedy Ellington, fondly referred to as "Duke." Ellington's was the background music of my growing up, the everpresent melody of life with Daddy. My father also listened to the music of Count Basie, Miles Davis, Dinah Washington, Coleman Hawkins, Monk, Mingus, Sarah Vaughn, Sonny Rollins, Gloria Lynn singing the hell out of "June Night," but invariably he returned to the Duke. Ellington's big band and the sound of his fingers on the piano was my bedtime lullaby. I heard Ellington mingled with the voices of my parents and their friends, the sound of ice tumbling and laughter, the women's high-pitched and sexy, the men's low and rumbling. Ellington drifted among the odor of the Haig and Haig Pinch, the scotch my father used to drink, provided counterpoint to the sound of footsteps as I lay in bed, trying to fall asleep amid the party noises. It was music for all occasions, for trimming the Christmas tree and opening birthday presents, for somber hours spent in front of the television watching the funerals of John F. Kennedy and Martin Luther King, Jr., hearing news of the murder of Malcolm X. Even now, when I hear "Take the A Train," or "Black, Brown and Beige," or "Sophisticated Lady," when I hear Ellington I am a young girl again, in my father's house, listening to the Duke and my father, hoping that he will turn to me, as the Duke often turned to his audience, and say elegantly and sincerely, "I love you madly."

It is not until I am a grown woman that my father explains to me the roots of his love for the Duke. "In 1929, when the Depression set in, my life changed from what it had been as a youth," my father says. "Before that, my father had been able to earn a good living, but then the Depression came, and things really didn't get better until the Second World War. Until then, there were no jobs, there was a lot of poverty and struggle, but there was also a real sense of family and community. You did not see a lot of affluence. There was no Social Security, no welfare. People were just out of work, out of thoughts, out of money. People in the black minority were not going to rise out of positions of service and servitude; your work was not rewarded, it was just taken." My father's already deep voice is deeper. I can hear the pain in it, see the shuffle, feel the rage that my father, the most unshuffling of men, must have felt.

"I remember being fourteen or fifteen and going down to Union Station in Washington to see Duke Ellington and his orchestra come off the train. They were so immaculate, they walked with their heads so high, looked so magnificent, that the way I thought of it was everything they wore was custom-made." My father's voice is light, rich, delight threaded through it. "Duke was sharper than the law allowed. Ellington, everyone in the orchestra, they held themselves as humans, as artists. They made an impression on me that I never lost sight of. Ellington's mystique, his artistry, from his bone marrow out, gave him a difference. He was so confident of himself, and the finest musicians in the world were a part of his orchestra. His presentation was always generous, he seemed to be devoid of ego, to have the capacity to see the other person first. Going to see Duke Ellington, I drank a cup of inspiration. That's what it was. A cup of inspiration."

Like my father, Ellington came from Washington, but from a middle-class family, and his father wanted him to be an artist. It is rare, then and now, for parents of any class to encourage a child to pursue a path so lacking in economic security. Even talented children are usually discouraged from pursuing the arts when it comes time to choose a career. The Duke was born in 1899, nearly one hundred years ago. Black Americans had been out of slavery little more than three decades and survival was of paramount importance. That his father urged him to be an artist is nothing short of amazing.

My father was born in 1916, in Washington, D.C. Like many of his peers, he was born poor to hardworking parents who never saw themselves firmly out of poverty. Born and raised in Virginia, both of my grandparents left school after fifth grade. My grandfather, Howard Nelson, met my grandmother, Florence Mills, in New York, in the first decade of this century. My grandfather was in New York working and my grandmother visiting relatives. They married in 1913 and moved to Washington, D.C., following the northern migration of thousands of southern, rural black folks from the farms of the South to the cities of the North in search of jobs and a better life. They had four children, three sons and a daughter, in rapid succession. My grandfather worked as a waiter in clubs, restaurants, oftentimes working on the road, traveling to where the work was. During the good times, he worked on the railroad as a dining car waiter, a job of great prestige in the early part of the century, work where a black man could make good tips and be treated with a little more dignity than most. My grandmother was a housewife until her children were of school age, then she went to work part-time in a school cafeteria. She was lucky; for most black women the only work available was as a domestic, cleaning up after white folks. For many women who migrated North "domestic service," as black people called it, was a route up and out of poverty, a step toward something better.

When the Depression came, my grandfather's income as a waiter fell abruptly and my grandmother's wages became the mainstay of the family. After the Depression, things were never as good again. My grandparents would be doing all right, and then something would come along: the failure of a business venture, a layoff, a family emergency, and they'd fall back into doing bad. Still, they never gave up, spent their whole lives trying to do better. They saw the education they'd been forced to abandon to earn a living wage as a permanent route out of poverty and insecurity for their children. Like so many beliefs, a central element in the foundation of theirs was fear: of poverty, of another Depression, of spending a lifetime trying to move forward, only to find themselves barely a few steps ahead of where they started.

I think my father was both motivated and haunted by their fear, afraid of reaching solid ground and then sliding backward, driven by the desire to permanently escape the fear, to be successful. Like many people who lived through the Depression, he lived in dread of the possibility of an abrupt fall from economic grace, consumed by the desire to insulate himself and his family from that possibility. He did that. But sometimes childhood nightmares and dreams are hard to let go of when you're grown. When you're little you'll be asleep and fall into a terrifying dream, you can't get fully awake, you're trapped in your own nightmare, but even so, you know you're going to wake up eventually, so you can kinda just grit your teeth and ride it out. When you're grown up, the nightmares aren't just there when you're asleep. Those are the ones that are hardest to escape from.

My father didn't dream boyhood dreams of being an artist or a dentist. He just wanted to be successful, have money, live well, walk with his head high, exude that "custom made" energy, that sense that everything fits perfectly. It is a sense almost impossible to reach if you are black in white America, where no matter what you achieve, the color of your skin is a permanent imperfection. My father says he enrolled in Howard University's Dental School during the early years of World War II because he'd heard that if you were in medical or dental school you wouldn't be drafted. But before that he had attended Howard as an undergraduate, and it was on campus that he met and mingled with the members of the black bourgeoisie he aspired to become a part of: young men his age who wore fine clothes, drove nice cars, laughed casually and without inhibition, moved in the world as if they had a right to the best it offered, who held their heads up and did not shuffle.

I do not think my father ever liked being a dentist. Nevertheless, as a man who demanded the best of everything, he strove to be the finest dentist possible. Dentistry was an available, lucrative way up and out in a world of limited possibilities, and he took it. Yet my father urged his four children not to follow in his footsteps and work all day with our fingers in other people's mouths. He wanted us to do better, be happier in our chosen vocation. He did not tell us what better is or how to get there, just that it was his expectation. Of his four children, three become artists, although my father had not encouraged this specifically as Ellington's father had.

In the 1930s, when my father was coming of age, American definitions of manhood were limited, proscribed, and segregated: for white men only. The dominant culture had few expectations of black men. If a black man simply stayed out of trouble, kept his head down, was suitably subservient and didn't bother white folks, he was a winner, an exemplary Negro. There was no expectation that a black person could, would, or should achieve anything. The notion that he could be on a par with or surpass white men was absurd. As did most men of his generation, my father found role models and the affirmation of possibility in the black community: in his tall, thick, cigar-smoking father with the walrus mustache, in a male teacher at Dunbar High School, Washington's most prestigious for Negro students, and in Duke Ellington.

It was not enough for my father to succeed in the black world that slavery created and segregation maintained, he wanted more, a bigger palette than one reduced to black and white. It was not enough to be the best Negro, or have the best Negroes could have, to be Number One in the Negro World. He did not want to succeed in an arena proscribed by race, his skin color serving as a permanent barrier to success in the wider world. My father wanted what white folks had, and then some, felt entitled to it. As my brother Stanley says, "Dad didn't want to be at the top of bourgie black people, he wanted to live like a white man." He did not want to be white, but to live as white, to have all that white folks had— including the luxury of being oblivious to color—without having to abandon his race.

Long before my father began competing in a predominantly white world, he lived in a black one. The darkest-skinned son in a family of light brown people, he grew up in Washington, D.C., where color prejudice among black people was more than a curious affectation. In the 1930s and 40s the correlation between achievement and skin color was real, and my father first fought the low expectations of other Negroes who could pass the paper bag test, proving themselves no darker than the familiar brown sacks, and thus worthy of acceptance. It was not so much that people overtly scorned my father as it was that they had few expectations of him. Poor and black, there was simply no reason to think that he would excel, distinguish himself, make it. My father told me that when he came home and told his mother he had enrolled in dental school, she laughed derisively, as if at something so absurd it was ridiculous.

My father got the last laugh. He became a dentist, was the most successful of his siblings, made it into the upper middle class. But for him and many fathers of his generation, the price of navigating the segregated road to success in the 1940s and 50s was defensiveness, a constant, smoldering rage, the loss of the ability to communicate love in any way but through material things. The closing of that opening, the soft spot in the soul, that allows us to give and receive love. I know this had much to do with being black and male, that sense that black men have of always moving through a world that is hostile, of constantly having to prove themselves non-threatening, intelligent, finally worthy of some small chance, while holding on to some sense of manhood. As often as not, by the time we saw my father he was so angry and exhausted from proving himself, posturing, holding his head so high his neck was stiff, that he had little to give. When I am grown and a parent myself, it comes to me that what my father wanted was for his family to replenish him with strokes and kudos, to show that we appreciated not only him, but the struggles he went through to provide the good life for us. I figure this out not because I am particularly sensitive to my father's needs way back when, but to my own needs in the here and now. I know what it is to sacrifice and work hard and sometimes eat crow in order to provide for family and never hear thank you. But unlike my father, I do not expect it, knowing that the nature of children is that they do not understand process and are ungrateful, and that that is one of the few freedoms of childhood, and as it should be.

I do not doubt that my father loved us, but because of the time, place, and circumstances of his life, his notion of love was inextricably bound to his accomplishments, his ability to strive, move forward, attain the good life. His wife, home, and children were reflections or accoutrements of his success, ornaments of his achievement, and expected to act accordingly. My father ruled us because it was the one place a black man was allowed to rule, where he could be sure of his hegemony, his authority. He wielded power in the family because it was where he could do so without overt risk, without seriously messing with the status quo by stepping outside his black world and touching upon white folks' sources of power. Most often, my father showed his love in intangible ways that to kids are frequently meaningless. I took living in a nice apartment, having pretty clothes, attending private school, and leaving the city during summer vacation for granted; I could not remember a time when we did not have these things. As a child, it did not occur to me to make the connection between the increasingly middle-class life I lived and the fact that my father was a dentist, worked hard, and was hard on us when he came home. I wanted my father to be home more often, give me more attention, and stop playing golf. In those ways he could show that he loved me, as my mother, who was with us, on us, and at us, did. I had no notion that my father, who seemed all-powerful and had ultimate authority, could not do everything, could not have it all, that the price of our economic security was in a pivotal way the emotional insecurity that resulted from my father's frequent absence and mercurial presence. As a young girl, I did not understand tough love, aloof love, unavailable love, or deferred love; these I have come to know intimately as a grown woman. A parent myself, I smother my daughter Misu with all the love I can summon, probably overdoing it just so she will never wonder if I loved her, will know how to recognize all kinds of love when it comes at her.

The price my father and many of his peers paid for professional, economic success is the absence, or maybe it is more accurately the atrophy, of the ability to express love in the small ways. The nuances—a hug, a glance, an hour randomly spent—that are most important and best remembered. Obsessed with the need to declare and prove his importance, to draw some invisible and impossible Maginot line which no one would dare cross, my father swept his four children and his wife into the service of his ego, his aims. We were expected to go along with the program. To act a certain way, accomplish specific things, achieve particular goals as refracted pieces of my father's actions, accomplishments, aspirations.

On Friday nights, when my father comes home, we wait in the hallway, watch the door, tremble with anticipation. Sometimes we will stand on the threshold and wait for the sound of the elevator, watch the number board as it ascends, hope it rises to the tenth floor, the top, opens, and then, Daddy! We run down the hall, my father hugs and kisses us, my mother's hair shimmers with streaks of silver as her neck drops back to kiss him.

At his best moments, my father is an adventurer, a lover of life, a man for whom the direct route is the one seldom taken. Going for rides with my father, we turn up roads marked with No Trespassing signs, meet odd people, climb over fences. Often we are busted but Daddy is so charming that no harm comes to us. Once, stopped for speeding in Pennsylvania on the way to Indianapolis to visit my mother's family, my father leaves the four of us and my mother in the car and drives off with the highway patrolman. We wait for hours by the side of the road, sometimes playing, sometimes bored, always worried. We learn early in life not to bug my mother by asking, "Where's Daddy? When's Daddy coming?" since she's as much in the dark as we are. When my father finally returns, he is laughing, ticketless. On the way to the station house my father has managed to charm the cop, who ends up taking him to lunch and wishing him Godspeed. The same dynamic operates in our family, in subtle ways. My father never has to take responsibility for his mistakes, the disappointments, his absence. He always manages to do exactly what he wants and make us love him more, thinking it will make him love us too. My father is unavailable, which makes me want him more. I live for many years believing these are the only terms on which women and men coexist.

I realize now that men are often given a pass that exempts them from the lives of their families. That my father missed the school play or never played ball with my brothers or did not really talk to his children or didn't come home and left us waiting with a fiftieth birthday cake, ice cream, and presents, passed by with the explanation—delivered by my present mother—that he was "busy" or "working hard for us," as if that explanation were good enough for us, or her. I know now that he certainly had to work hard to maintain the style of living that as a child I took for granted. The irony is that what we remember most from all his sacrifices and hard work are his absences. Even as adults, it is difficult to be grateful.

My father's charm and arrogance, his absolute certainty that he deserved the color-free best, is a defining element of his character. So is his rage at not getting it. He projected this onto his family, demanded that his children require the best and then kick ass if we didn't get it. My father took us out to dinner regularly to all kinds of restaurants, Syrian, Indian, Chinese, Italian. We learned which silverware went with what food and also how to eat with our fingers and chopsticks. Learned to study menus and wine lists and understand what was offered, to make the best choice. In girlhood, daunted by selections, I found refuge in the international commonality of duck, some incarnation of which seemed to be on most menus. It became a running joke between my father and I, and when the waiter turned to me and said, "And for the little lady?" my father would say, "She'll have the duck," and we would laugh together, wrapped in the warmth of our secret joke. But when the food arrived, the party was over. My father would interrogate each of us about the quality of our entree. Was the steak rare as ordered? The seasoning on the fish as requested? Rolls warm enough, shrimp appropriately chilled? "Because if it's not the way you want it, send it back!" my father would declare. "You're paying for it, and you should always get what you want." I understood that I could show my discerning taste by finding something wrong with my meal and sending it back. A few times I did just that, politely, as taught by my father. I gained not only my father's approval, but a profound feeling of power to be able, at ten, to ask for and receive things exactly the way I wanted them. It is exhilarating to be a child and command adults to do your bidding. It is far more difficult, but also more exhilarating, to accomplish this as an adult around issues more important than food.

In his eighth decade, long retired from a career that was a ladder into the upper middle class, that provided an income that enabled him to retire before he was sixty, that currently finances a spiritual quest that has taken him to study with Mahareshi Mahesh Yogi in Switzerland, to Muktanada's ashram in South Fallsburg, New York, and to India, my father would be defined by anyone's standards as "A Success." Yet it was never enough. For the last twenty years my father has been on a full-time search for spiritual enlightenment, something he pursues with the same vigor with which he sought material success, and with, in the end, the same lack of satisfaction. I think it was easy for both my father and those who lived with and were affected by him to assign the driven nature of his life, the endless searching and dissatisfaction, to race, but that is too simple, and makes of him too simple a man. As much as he was driven to simultaneously prove something because of his race and transcend it, my father was driven by his need to escape his class background and with it poverty, insecurity, and fear. There was, for him, always something better someplace else, up ahead, in the distance. What he attained was never enough or the best, and so he always wanted more. When I was fifteen, the year after he tried to throw the Christmas tree out the window, my father left his family. He went to work one day and didn't ever come back. Not to see his children, or explain, or make amends, not even to collect his wardrobe of fine suits, left hanging in his closet for what seemed like years, as if awaiting his return.

My father never came back. Not for his suits or his children. He also never got enough in the material world, and is still searching for spiritual fulfillment. He is not a man who is ever satisfied, and I have come to understand that his yearning and need and seeking has something, but not all, to do with race. When I ask him about his lifetime of simultaneous great achievement and enormous discontent, my father tells me a story.

"My father used to tell this story to me when I was growing up, and it established a way for me to view myself and the world," my father says. We sit at the kitchen table, my father dressed in red and white, his silver hair long, brushed back and into a short braid. He is living on an organic farm near San Diego, California, where he spends his days meditating and lying in the sun. His meals he takes directly from the earth, walking between rows picking and eating whatever strikes his fancy. Always different, an eccentric, someone who would go left rather than right, my father does not take refuge, as so many of his peers do, in the Christian church and its quid pro quo of heaven in exchange for true belief. My father does not turn West, but East. My father searches for spiritual enlightenment, release from the earthly bondage of karma and reincarnation, he seeks nirvana, the final beatific moment that transcends suffering, the elimination of desire and individual consciousness. Fasting regularly, eating little solid food, ingesting blue-green algae, my father says he wants to live forever and be light and ready for takeoff when humans learn to fly. Mostly, he lives in the world of the spirit, but every now and then he says something that reminds me that his feet remain on earth.

"In the South, these mean, evil crackers got ahold of a black man," my father says. "And instead of lynching him, they decided to dig a hole and put him in it, bury him up to his neck. Then they let Tag, a mean, hungry, drooling boxer, loose. So Tag ran back and forth and bit the black man, tore his head all up, ripped off an ear, urinated in his face, all kinds of things. Finally, as Tag ran over him yet again, the black man opened his mouth, grabbed Tag's balls, and bit down. Tag yelped and screamed and strained so hard to get away he pulled the black man clean out of the hole, and the man jumped up and escaped. And the white folks said, 'That nigger. Didn't even give old Tag a chance.' "

My father is in his eightieth year when he tells me this story. It defines the way he sees the material world: as fundamentally unfair, ultimately segregated, closed to him. Perhaps this is the source of much of my father's frustration, his anger when we were growing up. It must have been difficult to continue playing the game, knowing that he could never be the grand-prize winner. Maybe that's why he threw the Christmas tree out.

I was fourteen in 1966. We had left Harlem and moved downtown a few years earlier, were living on West End Avenue and 81st Street, had made it. When we moved, we left our old apartment virtually intact, taking with us only our clothes and a few treasured pieces of furniture my mother refused to leave behind. So few things were taken that someone entering the apartment after us would logically assume that we had simply gone out for the day, left, disappeared, not moved. It was as if my father shed the skin and life that he had been living and continued forward, into a new place, life, and identity, one untouched by the past. My father's life has been defined by similar departures. In 1954 he moved his dental office from a small building in Harlem, on 148th Street and St. Nicholas Avenue, to 30 Central Park South, right up the street from the Plaza Hotel. He says he moved downtown because he didn't want to do repair work, he wanted to create, do reconstructive dentistry. The move to an apartment downtown was jumping from the starter home to the luxury home, with no cumbersome baggage to remind him of the past and no stops in between.

No one really seems to know why my father threw the Christmas tree out. Because we got the tree on Christmas Eve, we usually didn't take it down until a week or so into the New Year, creating our own tradition to replace the one some follow that says the old tree goes out as the new year comes in. Maybe my father, in his office reconstructing teeth, building something new and beautiful in place of that which was old and rotted, was suddenly struck by the need for movement and rushed home, determined to get that damned tree out of his house. Maybe he'd asked my mother to take the tree down and she, busy with the four of us and reading a good book, didn't. My mother loves holidays, traditions, the tree. During holidays late at night I get up from bed and go into the living room and she'll be curled on the sofa, eyes open, the only illumination the blinking of the tree lights against her brown face.

My father does not stop and unplug the lights, but simply rips the tree down and drags it toward the window. The plugs, the wires torn out, remain in the sockets. My brother Stanley vividly remembers the noise, yelling, Daddy clutching the top of the tree and pulling it across the floor, the bulbs swinging madly, crashing to the floor, tinsel flying. Awakened by the noise, I stand in the doorway and watch my father freak out. He tries to push the tree out the window, but it is the biggest, best, cheapest tree, its branches are too wide to fit through the window. Cursing, he drags the tree across the parlor floor. Bulbs smash and garlands of beads roll across the floor like ball bearings as he heads toward the back service door off the kitchen. I cower, awestruck, held back by the force of his waves of rage.

"Why'd he do it?" I ask Stanley years later.

"Who knows? Dad was crazy," Stanley says.

"What he was saying? All I remember is being terrified and screaming 'No, Daddy, no!' and Leil yelling 'Stanley, Stanley!' and trying to stop him." My mother's name is A'Lelia. Leil is the nickname we give our mother after she and my father divorce, perhaps because in the absence of Dad we shy away from calling her Mom, another reminder of his absence.

"I think he was muttering something about 'Santa Claus is a white man, a white man,' " Stanley says. "But maybe I'm just imagining that. Have you asked Leil?"

I approach my mother cautiously. She is a no-nonsense, feisty little woman who brooks no bullshit and lives in the moment. The past she contemplates briefly, boxes into packages by category, and puts on the back shelf of her mind.

"Leil, remember the year Dad threw the tree out?" I ask.

"Of course. Who could forget."

"Why'd he do it?"

"How the hell do I know why your father does anything?"

"Do you think it was racism?"

"Racism?" My mother snorts. "What does racism have to do with it?"

"Maybe he'd had a hard day trying to make it, came home, saw the tree, something snapped, and he just went off." I volunteer a neat, explanatory scenario.

My mother laughs. "Well, he went off, all right. I don't know how much racism had to do with it."

"Well . . . What do you think it was?"

"Jill. Your father's crazy. You know that as well as I do. Maybe he'd been drinking. He's crazy. Why does he do most of the things he does? I'm sure it didn't have anything to do with us, or the Christmas tree. I don't know, and I wouldn't worry with it." End of discussion.

"Whatever it was I was feeling, that expression of it was only an expression of the anger that was in me, anger that had to do with something else," my father says when I ask him about it. "I guess my anger came from the worldly desires I had, and they're never placated, because there was always something else to want. I suppose it was an expression of pain."

When I grow up, it takes me years to admit I don't like the holiday season, a long, drawn-out affair that actually begins on Thanksgiving and lasts until after New Year's. I ascribe my negative feelings to not having any money, or not having been raised a Christian— this is one of the very few times I try and use this as a negative factor in my upbringing—or my progressive politics, or being anti-consumerism. But these are only minor elements. My discomfort with Christmas is rooted in my girlhood, in the strain of living with Daddy, of everything—including me—having to be perfect. Of the everpresent tension that built all year, so that by the time the holidays came our family's mandate was to be an idealized, living diorama attesting to Daddy's success, largesse, benevolent dictatorship. The price of not being these things, of not keeping up with Daddy's demands, was that we would be shoved into a closet and forgotten, or simply left as my father left his Harlem apartment, or offices, or, eventually, his family.

It is not only the result of chance or a shortage of available black men that I live most of my life alone and raise my daughter that way too. Loving men, I chafe at living with them, unable to be sure that I will not end up under their rule, subsumed, as I was by my father. As Misu gets older we shave Christmas down to its essence: a day everyone has off to get together and eat like the proverbial dogs. The families we have each created scarcely resemble the one I grew up in.

Now that my parents are divorced, my mother no longer waits until Christmas Eve to get the tree. This task no longer falls to the menfolk but to Stanley and me, who simply go out, find the nicest, biggest tree we can, and pay whatever's asked for it. My mother still bakes Russian tea cookies, black walnut and coconut cakes, several pies, which we scarf down even as we complain about fat and cholesterol, and go to the gym. When he is not somewhere in the world searching for the spiritual best, my father comes over for Christmas dinner. He is still the visitor, but, having abandoned us and his role as breadwinner and absolute authority so long ago, is no longer the patriarch. Over the years we have learned that what you see is what you get, that my father loves us to the best of his ability. Given this, we love him to the best of ours. Both the number of his expectations and the weight of his authority are diminished. My mother, the last traditionalist, holds court. She takes the tree down whenever she damn well pleases.

I BECAME A WOMAN for real on December 5, 1974, when I was twenty-two years old. On that day I found out that having periods, and breasts, and sleeping with men, and being able to make babies are just physiological technicalities, literal affirmations that you are female. These things don't have anything to do with figuring out how to *be* a woman. You have to find that out the hard way.

On a frigid afternoon in December 1974, New York Hospital, the hospital where I took my daughter to the pediatric clinic, detained me for prima facie child abuse and tried to take my daughter away. It was on that day that I began the process of understanding, not in an abstract, theoretical way but absolutely personally, what it can mean to be a woman, and a colored woman, and a poor colored woman in America. That there would be times when it meant that I was at the mercy of people who were none of those things. On that day it meant that they could take my baby girl away from me for fifteen hours and there was nothing, absolutely nothing, I could do about it.

"Prima facie" means "on the face of it," and on the face of it the hospital was concerned because my baby, her father, and I were on a macrobiotic diet, something they neither understood nor respected. I suspect all they saw was a young black woman on welfare and Medicaid, unmarried, presumably uneducated, who wouldn't obey the dictates of Western medicine. I refused to fill my daughter with vitamins, medication, and little jars of salted baby food. That I had other values and priorities didn't matter.

"We'd like the baby to stay overnight for observation," the doctor says.

"Is there something wrong?" I ask.

"We're not sure. That's what we want to find out."

"She's all right, isn't she?" I guess my voice sounds panicked, because the doctor, who's been speaking in a normal tone, switches to that slow, condescending, enunciating-every-syllable-of-every-word voice reserved for hysterical women and morons.

"Apparently, yes. But she's thin, not gaining weight as rapidly as I'd like, and in the bottom percentile of the chart on both weight and height. You have her on that diet," he says.

"A macrobiotic diet. We're on a macrobiotic diet," I say. "There's nothing wrong with that. I've been meeting with the hospital nutritionist regularly."

"I hope there's nothing wrong. We just want to be sure she's getting everything she needs. She's small, look at the other babies her age." He gestures toward several dozen children surrounding us in the pediatric clinic's waiting room. Around us, babies gurgle, cry, crawl on the floor playing with toys and each other. They are many sizes, shapes, colors. My daughter Misumbo, about to turn two in a few days, is among them. She is a tiny, delicate child, lean, perfectly shaped, with big, luminous eyes and a nearly bald head. If anything, it is her lack of hair, not her size, that worries me. I may not possess the-hair-is-a-woman's-crowning-glory mentality, still, I do not want my daughter to be forever bald. I am not comforted by older black women who tell me, "When a baby's bald like that, it means she's gonna have long, pretty hair, that good hair." Hey, I'd just like her to have some hair, good, bad, preferably indifferent.

My daughter and another little girl with thighs so fat she has to sling one over the other in order to walk, stand in the middle of the floor, each holding on to either side of a toy. "Mine!" the fat little girl shouts, tugging.

"We can share," Misumbo says.

"Mine!" the girl bellows, yanking hard, pulling Misumbo forward with the toy. She does not let go.

"We can both play," Misumbo says clearly. The little girl, red in the face and crying, shrieks, "NO!" and wrenches the toy toward her fat body. Misumbo lets go, falls backward onto the floor, looks around. Seeing me, she crawls over, climbs into my lap.

"But I've been working with the nutritionist, she says everything's fine." I stroke her baldie bean.

"But the nutritionist is not a doctor," he says dismissively. "We'd like to do some tests."

"What kind of tests?" Because we are on a macrobiotic diet, which in 1974 is seen as both daring and dangerous, I bring my daughter to the clinic once a month, where she's regularly tested. What more tests do these people need?

"Let's go upstairs and get her settled. Then we can talk," the doctor says.

"No. I've got to talk to her father first, he's working construction on the river, there're no telephones, I can't call him," I say calmly. "I'll talk to him tonight and bring her back tomorrow." Inside, I am freaking out, frightened that there is something wrong with my daughter that they won't tell me, that some horrible ordeal is about to begin and I just want to go home for one last night of peace and quiet before it commences. Besides, I know her father and I are in agreement: he wouldn't want me to leave the baby here all alone.

"It's important that we begin tests now," the doctor says, glancing down at the chart in his lap, his voice turned harsh. Am I paranoid, hearing things, or is he talking to me in that "Look you're just another young, unmarried, ignorant baby-making black woman in the Medicaid clinic so you'd better do what I say" voice? And there is no time to explain that I am intelligent, in college, working part-time, that I am on welfare to make ends meet and get health insurance for myself and the baby until I finish school, not unlike many women, then and now.

"I've got to talk to her father first," I say, hugging Misumbo. She squirms, puts her arms around my neck, holds on. I can feel her tiny, hot baby hands press against the tendon along the sides of my neck.

The doctor looks at me with disbelief, abruptly stands up. "I'll be right back."

I sit there for a few minutes and wait for him to return, then begin to slip my daughter's slender arms into the sleeves of her bulky jacket, trying not to panic. I'd started to cancel the clinic appointment this morning—had a bad feeling and just not felt like going—but then my Mommy-Jill, as my daughter sometimes calls me, that side took control. I didn't cancel but came anyway, because it was the right thing to do, and now here I am at the hospital with some doctor I've never seen before because Medicaid patients get whoever's on duty, telling me he wants to keep my baby overnight for anonymous "tests" and not telling me why.

I get Misumbo into her snowsuit and we sit there sweating in the windowless consultation room. She's pulling at the front of my coat, murmuring "Titty," because it's way past lunchtime. I'm struck by the irony of the hospital wanting to keep my daughter for tests because we're on a macrobiotic diet and theoretically depriving her of something, and at the same time making us miss snack time. Finally, tired of waiting, I decide to go home, feed the baby her organic rice cereal and mashed banana, nurse her, and put her down to wait for Byrd, her daddy, to come home. I stand up with the baby on my hip and walk to the door, but two big men swing across it from outside, sealing off my exit like the flapping doors of a saloon in a western just before the showdown. I say, "Pardon me," politely, expecting them to excuse themselves and step aside. Instead, one of them, a big, bulky guy who looks Puerto Rican and uncomfortable says, "Sorry, you can't leave."

Then everything speeds up into that crazy fast motion that always accompanies bad things, like fights and car accidents, events so accelerated they're almost indistinct except you know they're bad, bad, bad just from the little glimpse of all those negative occurrences whirling by. The doctor returns with a nutritionist and others on the hospital staff. We're all sealed in that tiny room with the swinging door security guards and one of the doctors tells me in a monotone, inhumanly calm voice like the one that announces floors on elevators that my daughter is underweight and not growing according to the expectations on "The Chart." Since I refused to leave her in their hands I'm being charged with prima facie child abuse which means that on the face of it, it looks to them like I might be abusing my daughter, and she's not going anywhere. A law recently enacted in New York enables hospitals to hold children they suspect are being physically abused by a parent or parents who bring them to the hospital beaten and bloody. Its purpose was not to detain the children of parents who adhere to non-traditional diets. I am the first person in New York City detained under this law.

All I can think is that my daughter's beautiful, healthy, talks in sentences, is willing to share toys, and doesn't have to fling one fat leg over the other to be ambulatory. I haven't seen any signs of red meat, Hostess Cupcake, or Gerber baby food deprivation. Ever since she was born I have been going to the hospital nutritionist regularly, I have read a dozen books on diet, sources of vitamins, minerals, proteins, food combining. I eat like a vegetarian pig to make sure my daughter gets plenty of good things from my milk. Why would I abuse her? I love her madly. I have even purchased a set of little bowls with lids into which I ladle rice, squash, rock-hard aduki beans that are a staple of a macrobiotic diet, fruit, bottles filled with homemade soy milk which takes hours to prepare, whatever foods my daughter should eat she gets, and lug them along when we go to visit friends or family, even though it would be easier to feed her whatever's available: baby food out of jars, Twinkies, Kool-Aid, staples of the all-American diet.

In the midst of the high-speed chorus of events and the music of bad, bad, bad, the only clear, steady thing is Misumbo, my responsibility. In the spring of 1972 at age nineteen, I told my family I was pregnant intentionally, in love but unmarried, and going to have the baby. I'd done one semester in college, was unemployed, living with a man named Byrd, my baby's father. My mother called one of the few family meetings I can remember, an indication of how concerned she was about my decision. My parents were separated by then, my father having deserted us abruptly when I was fifteen. As with so many divorces, with his departure my father lost most of his authority. He was instantly marginalized, on the periphery of his family's life, by choice on his part and self-defense on everyone else's. In his wake, my father left a brokenhearted woman, four traumatized teenagers, and an enduring sense of his absence. When he lived with us, even when he was not physically present he was there, my father's strength and arrogance and adventurousness, his mercurial nature, his unspecified anger, his standards, permeated not only the air but the cushions on the couch, drapes, oozed into our pores when we picked up a fork or glass. When he left, the essence that he left behind became stronger, even as his physical presence diminished, but it was spoiled, sour, we acknowledged but did not respect it. At the meeting about my pregnancy, my mother closed herself, my father, and me in the bedroom they once shared. We were imprisoned for several hours, during which my father didn't say much except to ask me if I was having the baby because of Nikki Giovanni, a poet who was a patient of his and had recently had a son without benefit of marriage. I liked her poetry, but it wasn't clear to me what the connection between me and Nikki Giovanni and our babies was, so I just said no. So my father clammed up, and then my mother went, "What the hell is the matter with you are you serious you're going to have a baby for what you're too young you've barely started college that goddamn Byrd I told you when you first started going out with him he was trouble and now you're pregnant have you thought about having an abortion I'll take care of it you have no idea what raising a child entails you are in for a big surprise I knew we shouldn't have sent you away to boarding school but your father . . ." Which went on for a couple of hours but didn't change my mind, in fact sitting there with my disappeared father and passionately in-your-face mother might have strengthened my resolve to make a better family on my very own to replace the one that vanished when Daddy left. After that evening my mother supported me unconditionally and has always adored Misumbo, her first grandchild, she is simply not a woman to hold her tongue. Anyway, now that I am a mother myself I can imagine her worry and rage, wanting me to have all the opportunities she did and more, and we were very, very middle class, educated, on our way someplace, and even though no one was quite sure where that was, it sure as hell wasn't to unwed motherhood at nineteen going on twenty.

I know now what my mother knew then, that having a child would increase the likelihood of my being poor, of being alone, of being dependent on welfare, food stamps, other support programs, of not finishing my education, of remaining unmarried, of perhaps having more children and with each birth increasing the odds that I would fall into a poverty difficult to escape. Now, when I recall her opposition to my pregnancy I marvel at her relative restraint, her calm knowledge in the face of my naive, youthful, and totally groundless surety.

I can see how bizarre and insane it must have seemed to my mother when I announced I was about to become a mommy. I'd barely been able to face the advent of menstruation eight years earlier.

"There's nothing to be scared or frightened about. It's natural. Congratulations, you're a woman now."

I look into my mother's face to see if she's kidding, has lost her mind, or turned into some perfect television clone mother à la June Cleaver, but she looks as she always does, normal. This is only momentarily reassuring, since I am eleven and have seen enough horror and science fiction movies to know there're plenty of organisms from outer space whose métier is alien reproduction of the human species. Maybe my mother's been possessed by the pod people.

She reaches out and strokes my hair. Her hand feels the same as it always does: warm, small, humanoid. "Do you have any questions you'd like to ask?" she inquires in the same soft, perfectly modulated voice she uses when she's tricking one of her four children, like when we go for checkups and she says, "Dr. Dobson isn't going to hurt you," moments before she holds me down and he jabs a needle into my butt so hard I can feel it strike bone.

I want to say, "Hell, yeah, I have some questions. There's blood seeping from between my legs, my panties are ruined, my stomach feels as if a giant fist is wringing it out, and I'm not supposed to be frightened? I'm terrified. Why is this happening to me, what did I do wrong? Even though you say sorry doesn't help maybe it will this time, I am really, really sorry, if I pray, will the bleeding stop?" But I don't.

"I have something for you," she says, reaching behind her. Even though I'm worried about my imminent demise, my heart leaps. A puppy! I'm finally getting a puppy! After years of begging and throwing tantrums without success, my dream is about to come true. I have a vision of myself lying dead in a pool of blood, my bereft puppy lapping frantically at my face. My mother hands me an enormous cardboard box. It emits no barks or yelps. On the side it says "Modess . . . *because.*" Because what? Why? What'd I do? "These are for you," she says. "To use when you're menstruating."

I hate that word, menstruating. Hate the way it looks, the way it sounds, how it's spelled, what it means. I am doomed to leak blood every month, consigned to wearing a sanitary napkin the width of a bath towel between my legs to soak it up. Everyone, too, will know I have IT, since it's clearly impossible to conceal the fact that I'm clenching a pad the size of a whole box of Kleenex between my legs. This absolutely cannot be happening to me.

"I don't think I need those," I tell my mother.

"Yes, you do. It's a little too early to start using tampons," my mother says. Tampons! Is she kidding? I'll be damned if I'm going to put one of those inside me, I might explode.

"I mean, I don't really think I'm doing it."

"Of course you are. There's blood, isn't there? Did you read the pamphlet Dr. Dobson gave you?"

The pamphlets, right. White and pale pink for my sister and me, blue and white for my brothers. Why is it that pink is the universal symbol for girl stuff, the color of washed-out bloodstains? I've never liked pink.

"Yeah, but there was blood before, and it went away." A few months before, I'd come home from school and noticed red stuff in the crotch of my panties. I must admit that it occurred to me that maybe I'd started menstruating, but I dismissed the thought. It wasn't that I was stupid; I knew what menstruating was, I just wasn't ready for it to happen to me. I thought if I ignored it maybe it'd just go away. Obviously, my strategy didn't work.

"Jill. Are you all right?" my mother asks kindly.

"No. This is horrible." My mother wipes my face, hands me the napkin and belt, points me toward the bathroom.

"Mom," I wail.

"Go ahead. You can do it. You're a woman now," she says. She's smiling, but those tears still balance, tottering, on the rims of her eyes. I have no idea what she's talking about. Menstruation technically confirms that I'm female, can have babies. That doesn't tell me anything about what being a woman is or how to become one.

The early 1970s were the beginning of a wake of many years, a communal, cold-turkey withdrawal from the political and cultural highs of the 1960s. What is true for many of us who were teenagers, dependents of our parents, in the 1960s, is that we were too young to go on the freedom rides or be drafted so that we could resist, to accompany Jane Fonda on a fact-finding mission to Vietnam, or join the Black Panther Party. We were involved in supporting roles as demonstrators, or envelope stuffers, or placard carriers during the battles for civil rights, women's rights, against the war in Vietnam, for the liberation of political prisoners, to stop police brutality. We were into it, but not really of it, believed in the need for social change but didn't truly understand the absolute necessity of fundamentally transforming society. We were revolutionaries in training, relegated by our age to the role of supporting players. By the time we were old enough to take over the lead, the play was closing. Our ability to imagine the world that could be far outstripped our understanding of what was necessary to truly transform America. So when the going got tough in the late 60s and early 70s, too many of us got going, literally. Into our whiteness, our middle classness, our trust funds, an anachronistic nationalism, our privilege of birth, or, as I did, the privilege of giving birth.

Coming down from the high of the 1960s, I was confused and searching when I met Byrd, the man who would become my daughter's father, at a party the summer of 1971. It was late, I was sweating from dancing, and on my way to the bathroom because the year's big slow grind, the Jackson Five's "Never Can Say Goodbye," had just come on. I was bogarting my way through the crowd to avoid being dry-humped by some man I'd never seen before and didn't want to see again. Between 1965 and 1975 I heard most slow songs only dimly, through bathroom doors, laying low until I heard a fast beat and it was safe to come out.

There was a line outside the bathroom, so I leaned against the wall to wait, a safe place since even the most desperate of men, the ones who go down the line of women at a party, sweaty hand outstretched in the near darkness, indiscriminately asking everyone to dance, even these men know better than to mess with women waiting outside the bathroom. I stood there watching the couples on the dance floor, pelvises clenched together, hips grinding, one man's bent leg pushing deeper between a woman's thighs as a youthful Michael Jackson—before superstardom, Neverland, Liz Taylor as his very best friend, accusations of pedophilia, marriage to and divorce from Elvis's daughter, or fatherhood—crooned, and then I saw him. Medium height, thin, with a small, elfin, sort of pointed face and a round, perfect Afro standing six inches out from his head. He wasn't dancing, he was just standing there in the center of the dance floor, wearing a white short-sleeved shirt, skintight pink satin pants, leaning on a cane with a silver head, looking dead into me with liquid brown eyes. What can I say? I never made it into the bathroom. Next thing I knew we were on the dance floor, grinding away. I think slow dances are a prelude to sex, a dry run. I was nineteen, had just started college, was unattached. Byrd was eccentric, spiritual, smart, visually arresting, and he had that certainty that some men are born with or cultivate, the sense that he knew something wonderful the rest of us didn't. I was still young enough to believe that when a man's dick got hard it was a personal compliment. I have since learned that more often it's simply a knee-jerk reaction to poontang proximity.

Our daughter was conceived early in 1972 to the number-one rhythm of Al Green's "Let's Stay Together." I think I fell in love with Byrd and Al Green's romantic lyrics simultaneously, as if they were one and the same. There was something sincere about Al's crooning, his velvety, approachable voice. He even looked sincere, not super-fine like he'd be nothing but heartache, but good-looking enough that he'd keep you satisfied. Green has the face of a man who knows how to fix things around the house, stereos and small appliances, one of those sincere, do right man faces, attractive but not too pretty. It's the pretty men who don't know how to fix shit, say they do, and leave smoke coming out of the toaster and your speakers blown out. There are probably thousands of young people in their early twenties who were conceived to the sound of Al Green. Music is so defining of moments. It could have been worse, the other number-one songs in 1972 were "Papa Was a Rollin' Stone," the Temptations ode to a dysfunctional family, "My Ding-A-Ling," Chuck Berry's homage to his penis, and Billy Paul's "Me and Mrs. Jones," about an adulterous affair.

We lived together in an apartment in Harlem, and on every other block there was a cramped record store with beat-up speakers set up out on the sidewalk specializing in cubbyholes full of 45 rpms blaring "Let's Stay Together." We used to walk down Broadway from 157th Street where we lived and that's all we heard, Let's Stay Together, Let's Stay Together, Let's Stay Together, we could sing along from block to block, Let's Stay Together, that was our mantra, so in love were we two and making a baby seemed right and inevitable, an act of affirmation and life in the midst of the extended death throes of the 1960s.

By 1975 Byrd and I had separated. Al Green and Michael Jackson didn't live up to the promises of their romantic lyrics, either. In October of 1974 in Memphis, Tennessee, a woman named Mary Woodson threw a pan of scalding grits on Al as he was climbing out of the bathtub, after which she shot herself, leaving behind a suicide note addressed to the crooner. Shortly thereafter, Al renounced singing those lusty grind 'em ups, became a minister, and thereafter sung no more songs in praise of love, lust, or sex, but in praise of the Lord. Given the choice of a hot grits bath and religious conversion or being a single mother going to college with a baby strapped on my back, I think I did all right. Sometimes, though, I miss believing in those love songs. Neither Michael Jackson singing "Never Can Say Good-bye" or Al Green crooning "Let's Stay Together" managed to keep Byrd and me united. Just as the songs faded from the airwaves, the love vibe they'd woven around us wafted away too, unable to be heard above the demands of being young, a mother, black, poor, and female in the political culture of America in the early 1970s. By 1975, the charges filed against me the previous year for alleged child abuse had made it clear how vulnerable I was, how tenuous not only my life, but the life I was trying to make for my daughter actually was. I suddenly saw the demons of poverty and dependence and helplessness, the ones my mother spied hovering around me when I was still pregnant. Now, they were so close I could smell their fetid breath. I think that Byrd felt this vulnerability, this potential for absolute powerlessness looming outside our door as strongly as I did; it was the response we couldn't agree on. He believed that we could turn inward, create a family and a world of our own making inside our apartment, exist simultaneously in America but not of it. I did not think this would work, but thought instead that the answer was to arm myself with skills, ideas, understanding, an active politic. I wanted to get out in America and fight. I knew that being poor and uneducated and on welfare dramatically increased my chances of being victimized, and I was no longer optimistic about the ability of family alone to protect and overcome.

But at the hospital nothing is clear, the world is trembling and all I can think of is that I'm still nursing but they've taken Misu away and my breasts are hard like rocks, filled up and leaking, and I've got to focus, protect my daughter, not fail her and confirm everyone's worst fears, and my own, that I'm not ready enough, responsible enough, old enough, not woman enough, to be a mother. In an instant the doctors, the nutritionist, the hospital personnel who were sometimes helpful and generally harmless have become dangerous, enemies, they have stolen away my naïveté and revealed themselves as people from whom it is my responsibility to protect my daughter. So I do the only thing I can think of to do: I call my mommy and daddy, then everyone else I know who might be able to help me.

The saving grace about most families is that whatever the internecine battles, in a crisis they usually manage to overcome it, at least temporarily. My parents are acrimoniously separated, but not divorced. My father lives on Martha's Vineyard with his latest girl-friend, searching—late—for the hippie experience. My parents do not have what could be described as a good working relationship. But when they learn New York Hospital is trying to take away their only grandchild, they temporarily drop all weapons and focus on protecting the baby. My mother, an omnivore who eats every-thing and thinks I'm crazy to have her grandchild on a macrobiotic diet, utters not one word of I-told-you-so, entertains not a moment of doubt—or maybe she does entertain them, but she sure as hell doesn't speak them. She simply begins contacting every doctor, ad-ministrator, and city official she knows.

In the end I get Misumbo back, intact, although we are fright-ened in the middle of the night when a hospital worker tries to wheel her bed to that place where hospitals perform "tests," the specifics of which are vague since the only one they mention is a spinal fluid tap, which sounds horrendous. Luckily, he clumsily rams the corner of the bed into the door frame, awakening not the baby but her slumbering father, who prevents their exit.

The following morning my family meets with a battery of doc-tors who look as if they have been caught amputating the wrong foot, when what they were really doing was just as bad: trying to run some doctor-knows-best line on another poor, colored woman alone, the perfect victim. Only this time, on this rare occasion, they get their fingers caught up in the vise of our middle-class, edu-cated, black rage. And here class is the important thing—my par-ents', not mine, since I am poor. But they are educated, professional, successful, it is they who have called friends at all hours, explained, cajoled, pleaded, begged them to call the hospital and tell them to let my daughter go. Without them, I do not know what might have happened. Later, I hear horror stories: A light-skinned, blonde toddler wanders away from her brown-skinned mother in the subway, the police find her. When her brown mother attempts to reclaim her child, the police will not believe she could have birthed the baby. They take her to a hospital for tests; when the mother finally gets to her hours later, the little girl is dead.

We sit in a room full of doctors that morning, my daughter on my lap. They mouth conciliatory sentiments that are false. I look in their faces and maybe I'm having an acid flashback because they all appear monstrous, but I don't think I'm tripping: it's their true colors shining through. Fed up and frightened, I finally get up in the middle of their blah, blah, blah, put Misu on my hip, and walk to the door. I don't plan to, but suddenly I start yelling, cursing them out, I can't help myself, I'm a fool in love you see—in love with my daughter. Then I kick over an incubator or some contraption, and leave. When my parents meet me at the elevator a few minutes later, neither one of them says a word about my behavior or tells me I was being dramatic.

Outside the hospital, in the cold, I clutch my darling daughter to milk-swollen breasts, rock steady, hold on against the hurricane force created by the realization of the precariousness of our existence, that scant moment in which, if you are female, poor, black, young, or all of the above, you can become, instantly, rendered vulnerable. I now realize that strangers who know and care nothing about me can step into my life and alter it as irrevocably as having a child altered mine. It is then, in December of 1974, that I first understand what it means to be a woman in this culture, to know my responsibility and this terrible vulnerability and that there are passages of relief but really no escape from either.

My mother hugs me in the cool, bright December sunlight, the baby squished between us, happy and squirming. When she pulls away, my mother's face is smooth, calm. It is only around the edges of her mouth, eyes, her forehead, that there are those other lines I have seen before but never recognized until now, wrinkles of rage and sorrow. When she looks at Misu's smiling face and smiles back, they disappear, at least for a moment.

Congratulations, I'm a woman now.

SLAVES IN LOVE

THERE IS SO MUCH MISCOMMUNICATION, hostility, and some-times even hatred between black women and men that I've taken to reminding myself that I love men. Not only in the abstract—I have a litany. I repeat to myself the names of beloved men: my father, un-cles, my brothers, men I'm friends with, men I work with, men I've slept with, men I haven't met yet but know I'm going to. For black Americans, the tension between women and men is exacerbated by our collective history, willful amnesia, and dangerous silence when it comes to the central and defining event of our lives, slavery. Cou-pled with the racial hatred that not only surrounds us, but too often has been internalized and emanates from us, the dismal state of af-fairs between black women and men should come as no surprise. It's hard to hold on to your humanity, your ability to love, when the na-tional psyche is so profoundly invested in defining black people as always part of the problem, rarely part of the solution.

Until we begin to understand the institution of slavery and its encompassing and continuing effect on all of us, there is no way that we can begin to love ourselves or each other. We cannot forget that we were in slavery longer than we have been out of it. Slavery was not something that happened and went away; it was comprehensive, and its effects are still manifest. Its goal may have been exploitation of labor, but the process of achieving that goal involved destruction of language, culture, history, religion, political systems, and family. Why would we think that after in excess of two hundred years living in slavery that when emancipation came black people could simply walk away from the plantation, physically free and psychologically unaffected?

The first time I met Mtume, a composer and political artist who has been involved in most of the major musical and political movements of the last thirty years and now scores the television show "New York Undercover," he got in my face and said, "We're going to be friends for a long time, so let's really talk." Inevitably, the subject got around to women and men, and I asked him, "What's wrong with the brothers?" not really expecting an answer, and he said, "The trouble with black men is that we've never forgiven ourselves for not defending black women and children during slavery, for punking out. And black women are still mad at us for not taking care of you all on the plantation."

I have thought about Mtume's words a lot. I think what he says is true to the extent that many black people believe slavery existed and persisted for as long as it did because of some failure of will on our parts. The false perception that if we'd just been stronger and more courageous we would not have been enslaved. The false perceptions that slavery "wasn't that bad," and that if black people had just been able to more effectively embrace the patriarchal role of men as protector and women as protected, everything would have been different. These perceptions linger in our collective consciousness because we refuse to read, think, or talk about slavery and its continuing effects. We relegate our history of enslavement to the unpleasant past and pretend that we no longer suffer from its effects except, occasionally, when assigning blame.

The literature of slavery is eloquent and extensive in documenting the efforts of slave couples to hold families and relationships together in a situation in which their ability to provide for, defend, and protect one another was nonexistent. When this was impossible the concept of extended family was invoked to create family units in response to the separations of the slave system. The notion that slaves were devoid of family structures and sexually wanton has been firmly debunked by historians. In spite of the efforts of slaves to maintain familial ties, the ultimate authority was always the master, and slaves had no institution that he was required to respect. If he chose to sell a slave woman's children or sleep with a male slave's wife, there was literally nothing that could be done about it, although some died trying. As troubling as the notion that slavery prospered for as long as it did as the result of some inherent weakness on the part of the enslaved is the idea that if black men had been more effective patriarchs the situation would have been changed in some fundamental way. In fact, to a significant extent, patriarchy was the bone thrown to black men after emancipation by both the government and the white Christian church. As Dr. Donna L. Franklin writes in her fascinating book *Ensuring Inequality: The Structural Transformation of the African-American Family,* "Although historians have generally agreed that black males and females were rendered equally powerless during slavery, there has been less emphasis on the fact that emancipation was followed by attempts to establish the black man's patriarchal authority within the family." Franklin details how, post-emancipation, black men were given the right to sign labor contracts for the entire family and were paid more than black women for the same labor, and smaller land grants were given to households headed by women. She also documents the ways in which the white Christian church encouraged the rise of patriarchy in black families, to the detriment of black women.

It may be a tired old saying that "those who don't know their history are doomed to repeat it," but that doesn't make it any less true. As a group, black Americans are fundamentally ahistorical when it comes to the longest and most important period in our history, slavery. With the exception of history classes and special interest groups, we don't talk about slavery. Even in the above contexts, when we do discuss slavery it is most often briefly, in terms of inspirational highlights, kind of the "Great Slaves of Yore" take on our collective history. Frederick Douglass, Harriet Tubman, Nat Turner, Denmark Vesey, rebellious slaves who either liberated themselves or died trying we can cope with, stand to hear about, dare to mention. Even Sally Hemings, a slave woman owned by President Thomas Jefferson who bore him several illegitimate children, is a safe topic for discussion, as if Hemings' reputed mulatto beauty and alleged "love affair" with Massa lifted her above the rank of your ordinary, run-of-the-mill beast of burden, better living through slavery. But these women and men were exceptions to the rule. The truth is that just as most of our ancestors in Africa were not kings or queens but workers, most of our slave ancestors weren't Kunta Kinte, Harriet Tubman, or Frederick Douglass, but ordinary slaves who worked the fields, were physically assaulted at the whim of the master, bore mulatto children as the result of rape, lived lives in which force, dehumanization, and reduction to the status of animals were the cornerstones of maintenance of the system of slavery. This is not to say that untold slaves did not have the potential to develop the intellect of a Douglass, the courage of a Harriet Tubman, or the rage for freedom of a Nat Turner, but that the absolutely oppressive system of slavery worked to keep the vast majority of that potential suppressed. We need to face the obvious and simple fact that American slavery was the most exploitative and oppressive system on earth, in all its particulars, not something that happened to African people because we were cursed, or weak, or chickenshit, or not men or women enough to do something about it.

How can we understand and overcome the effects of slavery if we don't talk about it, don't read about it, and generally don't seem to want to know? Most of our knowledge of slavery comes from novels, Hollywood, and television, to our detriment. Happy Mammy in *Gone with the Wind,* who chose to stay with Miss Scarlet after emancipation. Or how about the miniseries made from Alex Haley's *Roots* (produced and directed by whites), in which slave women wore neat calico dresses, nary a raggedy slave man could be found, and slaves mated over dinner dates down in the quarters, during which chicken—doubtless fried—was served? Or *Queenie,* a TV movie made from Haley's posthumously published novel (completed, by the way, by a white man), in which Hallie Berry played the beautiful slave mulatrix engaged in what we were asked to believe was a mutual, deep, sustaining love affair with Massa. Spare us. As my friend Antoine says, "The plantation wasn't a country club, it was where they beat you with a club." This is bad and dangerous history. What it posits is not simply that love can exist and blossom in a relationship based upon literal ownership of black women, whose primary function was to produce more slaves, but, more insidiously, that black women both enjoyed and benefited from slavery. Black women as beneficiaries of and colluders in their own and black men's oppression.

These entertainment products have little to do with reality or history, but serve three crucial ends: they make money; in their dishonest efforts to put a "human" face on slavery, they make white people feel better; and they suggest that black women through our opportunism and black men through failure to assert their male authority colluded in our enslavement. Yes, yes, of course we know some of those Massas weren't very nice people, I mean, did Kunta really deserve to have his foot chopped off, and it wasn't right to sell those cute pickaninny chillen down de river. But there's a flip side, just look at the happy darkies fiddling, mating, dancing, sometimes even trying to escape, occasionally falling in love with their white rapists. The subtext of this putting a happy face on slavery is always the same: Slavery really wasn't all that bad. Slaves were, after all, ignorant heathens, animalistic, probably couldn't have made it out there on their own, needed to be civilized, Christianized by a bunch of zealots and losers who were run out of England on a rail, slavery as problematic but benevolent institution.

In part because we embrace a collective amnesia about slavery, the major representations of the initial and still defining event of our history in North America come from white people, the descendants of the ones who created and enforced our enslavement. Can you imagine the Jews allowing the descendants of Hitler, Goebbels, and Eichmann to write their history? Is it any wonder that these representations are distortions: happy nigrahs, manicured, lush cotton fields, bare bones but cozy slave shacks, fly slaves? We need to get over denial of our collective history of slavery, and then avidly read, talk, watch, and listen to find out what it was really about. Haile Gerima's wonderful film *Sankofa* is a first step. On this plantation there are no cane fields laid out like English gardens, no benevolent Massa, no cheerful pickaninnys in sight. Gerima offers us the real deal: back-breaking labor, suffocating heat, constant brutalization. What slave life was like and what it did to the bodies, spirits and psyches of Africans and their African American descendants. Then, go to the library. For starters, read John Hope Franklin's *From Slavery to Freedom,* Na'im Akbar's *Chains and Images of Psychological Slavery,* and Toni Morrison's *Beloved.*

Most of us do not read, think, or talk about our history in slavery or its effect on our present. We deny its impact, buy whole hog into who America says we were then and who we are now, as if where we came from, how we got here, and what has transpired during our tenure in America is irrelevant. Oddly, while we are willing to give credence to how slavery transformed white people, their racist attitudes, racial imperialism, and racial hatred, we refuse to consider the subtle ways it's distorted our sense of ourselves as black women and men. Our own color complexes, our classism, our materialism, what we find valuable or beautiful, our aspirations and sense of possibility. The construct of the emasculated, undervalued, beaten-down black man and the fecund, seductive, opportunistic black woman in slavery has been repeated so often that we have come to accept it as true. Rather than understand that women and men were equally oppressed during slavery, though in different ways, we have bought into the falsehood that black women were better off, and that the level of black men's brutalization was a result of this. To believe that black women "got over" during slavery at the expense of black men is to absolve white people of accountability for slavery and lay that responsibility at the feet of black women. This done, it is no stretch to believe that the role of black women post-slavery is to repair the greater damage done to black men, to make up for our past imagined sins.

The ways we are portrayed in mass culture have a profound influence on the ways we view ourselves and each other. Overwhelmingly, black male slaves are portrayed as violent, menacing, ineffectual beasts of burden, their purpose to work the field and function as plantation stud, producing slaves, or objects of ridicule.

At best, a black man might be Massa's loyal retainer: wise, thoughtful, and intimidated, Uncle Tom. Black women are portrayed as either broad-breasted, ever-suckling, long-suffering, biscuit-baking Mammys, or as dusky, sloe-eyed temptresses unable or unwilling to resist the nocturnal advances of the white man. Current images in the culture, particularly in films and music videos, of young black men as angry, violent psychopaths who will get you with either their gun or their penis, and black women as skeazin' hos or long-suffering doormats, are nothing more than a contemporary update of the same tired, debilitating, hateful representations. The tragedy is that these images have been repeated so often and for so long that we've begun to believe that they're real. That we are who television, sentimental fiction, music videos, and movies say we are. Sadly, the consequence is that much of the hostility between black men and women has little to do with reality, but is essentially a case of warring representations.

In our interaction with the larger white culture, in ways obvious and subtle, the legacy of slavery and continuing racism informs all our transactions. In one shop a salesperson does not notice me at all, I am unimportant and invisible, surely not a viable customer. In another the clerk stalks me from aisle to aisle, watching closely to make sure I do not steal anything. I note the tensing of bodies when a black man, particularly a young one, enters an elevator, see it in the hand that switches a pocketbook to the opposite shoulder when a brother passes by. When I go to work it is communicated to me that I have to make myself "less black"—whatever that means at a given moment—so that white people will be able to deal with me. There is no corollary pressure on white people to make themselves "less white," so black people may better deal with them. Comparably, mistakes made by one black person reflect negatively on the entire race, while success accrues only to the individual. When we hear news of a sensational crime we immediately hope that the perpetrator is not black, because if he or she is we know that white people, and we, believe that it reflects negatively on all of us.

Sometimes I think the worst part of living in a culture entrenched in racism and racial hatred is the constant wondering. Did I not get the job, was my call not returned, did the restaurant put me at the table next to the kitchen, pay me less, not include me, shortchange me, did the police stop me, because I'm black? After a while, the wondering becomes as powerful as the knowing. If you have a day in which you do not, overtly or covertly, encounter racism, you feel lucky. The sad truth is that sometimes it's enough that no one said or did anything negative to you; positive actions don't even figure into the equation. Even with a brief respite, you never really escape, since being a member of an easily identified and nationally loathed racial minority seeps into your pores, gets in your bloodstream and your psyche. Once the seed of black hatred is planted, it grows, fed with regularity by politicians, newspapers, magazines, television, pundits, casually and unthinkingly by the average white person on the street who either does not see you or sees you only as a threat, it matures into self-hatred. If the signals I get from the dominant culture are that I am a person deserving of disdain, is it any wonder I begin to hate myself?

But self-hatred manifests in much more private, everyday ways for most of us. When we look in the mirror and are fundamentally and inherently unhappy with those racial aspects of what we see reflected there, whether hair or nose or skin color or body type. When we find ourselves seeking out doctors, lawyers, and other professionals who are not black, as if blackness were some immutable flaw to professionalism. Carrying around the albatross of hatred and self-hatred, some folks implode. Others explode and get violent, like Colin Ferguson, who got on the Long Island Railroad in 1994 with a semiautomatic weapon and started shooting white people, killing six. Most of us do neither. Instead, we carry the burden of racial hatred and self-hatred around with us as we function, do our best, try and live a decent, and maybe even happy, life. Our self-hatred is like a leaky faucet: unnoticed or commented upon but still corrosive. We may subconsciously seek to expel that self-hatred in order to avoid internal combustion. We seek the closest target outside ourselves: other black people. In a sexist, patriarchal society, in which one of the few areas of authority black men are allowed is over black women, this has devastating effect.

Not long ago, a martini-drinking man initiated a conversation with me in a bar while we were each waiting to meet someone else. Of course, the conversation turned to women and men.

"I don't date black women," the man proudly slurs.

I start to say, "Well, I don't date drunks, so we're even," but don't. I'm curious to find out what he has against sisters, so instead I say, "Oh really," hoping to draw him out.

"Yep. I used to, but not anymore," he says, leaning toward me conspiratorially. His breath is pure vodka.

"Why's that?"

"Too hard, too mean, too demanding," he whispers, then adds, "No offense to you," although how I could avoid offense is beyond me.

"In what way?"

"You know how you sisters are," he snarls. "Always in a man's face, got something to say about everything." He gulps his drink.

"Maybe it's not black women you're not interested in. Maybe it's that you don't want an equal partner," I suggest. He looks at me, then looks away, toward the door. Relief slides across his flushed face.

"Well, here's my date. Nice talking to you." He doesn't sound sincere. I follow his eyes and see a woman approximately the color of milk chocolate with shoulder-length straightened hair walking toward us. She is wearing a suit, stockings, and sneakers, looks like a million black women after a hard day at work.

"That's your date?" I ask. He nods. "I thought you didn't date black women," I say. He throws back the rest of his drink, rises to meet her.

"She's not black. She's West Indian," he says, and walks away.

For black women to publicly examine the crisis between black women and men is most often seen as an attack upon and betrayal of black men. Ntozake Shange was condemned for writing the choreo-poem *for colored girls who've considered suicide when the rainbow is enuf* in 1975, with its critical portrayal of men's treatment of women. Alice Walker was tarred, feathered, and damn near run out of the race on a phallic rail when her Pulitzer Prize–winning novel *The Color Purple,* with its chilling portrait of the brutal black man "Mister," was published in 1982, followed by the Steven Spielberg movie in 1985. And let us not forget that both these works were classified as fiction. The vicious reviews, endless round table discussions, panels, columns, and conversations, in which many men proudly prefaced their ranting with the declaration that they hadn't read the book or seen the movie, as if this were some badge of righteousness, made it clear that critiquing black men, even in fiction, was unacceptable. But if you're looking for the ultimate example of effective damnation and racial expulsion for speaking publicly about the state of affairs between black men and women, look no further than the vicious and long-lived criticism in response to the publication in 1979 of Michelle Wallace's book of essays on the problems between black women and men, *Black Macho and the Myth of the Superwoman.* Reaction to Wallace's book made it clear: Not only do black women have no right whatsoever to criticize black men, if they do every attempt will be made to beat them into the ground.

Such response and censure has a chilling effect not only on the specific women attacked but on all black women. Already effectively marginalized from mainstream culture, how devastating for a black woman to be cast out of the race too, for the crime of daring to speak the truth as she perceives it.

I'm hard-pressed to think of any instance in which a black male's portrayal of black women, however negative, brutal, or misogynistic, resulted in an outcry even approximating that aimed at black women. Not *Native Son,* in which Richard Wright's fictional Bigger Thomas casually kills his black girlfriend and throws her body away, or, nearly fifty years later, Nathan McCall's autobiographical *Makes Me Wanna Holler,* in which he recounts participating in "trains," gang rapes of young black girls. Clearly the standards for critique are different for men and women. Where black men are hailed for their realism and for tellin' dos' hard ghetto truths, black women are attacked and discredited professionally and personally if we dare to serve up our own reality about black men.

Whatever the genre, black women are fair game. It is a tradition among many black male comedians to dress up as black women, transforming themselves into objects of revulsion and ridicule. From Flip Wilson in the 1970s in drag playing loud, crass, unattractive "Geraldine" (whose boyfriend was, not insignificantly, named "Killer") to the contemporary situation comedy "Martin," starring Martin Lawrence, whose drag alter ego is an ignorant, loud, sexual predator named Sheneneh, the way to elicit a guaranteed laugh is to put on a dress and play the unattractive, dominating, sexually voracious black woman. Black male comedians have encased black women in a negative stereotype, the basis of which is self-hatred projected on the handiest target: black women.

Even when the representations of black women are not as overtly demeaning as those of male comedians in drag, they are no less disturbing, and possibly more dangerous, since they often seem "normal." Louise Jefferson, the character played by Isabel Sanford in the situation comedy "The Jeffersons," about an upwardly mobile black family, which ran from 1975 to 1985, is a well-dressed, nicely coifed, upper-class representation of black woman as emasculating matriarch, ruling the roost and keeping not only her incompetent, cocky little husband in line, but her evil, trickster maid too. On the big screen, Spike Lee's Nola Darling in his debut film *She's Gotta Have It* is a black man's postmodern spin on the construct of black woman as opportunistic, amoral sexual predator. Juggling intimate relationships with three men simultaneously, Nola may appear to be the liberated woman of the 1980s—until, that is, she is forcibly sodomized by one of her lovers (interestingly, until then the one most likely to be nominated a "Nice Guy"). This event enables her to see the error of her ways and settle down, presumably to live happily ever after, with her assailant.

More recently, in the contemporary situation comedy "Living Single," about four young black women in New York, the representations of black women, while more sophisticated and charming than most we've seen in the past, are not that far from their negative and negating predecessors. There's dark-skinned Max, the loud-mouthed, emasculating black bitch; Regine, the dusky mulatto seductress; Synclaire, the empty-headed buffoon; and finally Khadijah, a hip, updated version of that old black matriarch. It should be noted that the only woman who has a steady man is Synclaire, the ditz who functions as straight woman.

Most representations of black women in popular culture stem from the slave roots of Mammy or Mulatto, often developing their own bizarre hybrid. Dark-complected Sheneneh on "Martin," played by Lawrence in drag, may be the hideous, unattractive, class-less extreme, but both light-skinned Gina, Martin's wife, and Pam, her brown-skinned best friend, are part of the same continuum. Gina is the middle-class version of the same stereotype, her shrill, emasculating shrewishness toned down, tucked into a suit and a job, recast as annoying but ever faithful and wise enough to know when to be subservient supporter of her black man. Pam is the working-class incarnation: the oversexed bitch, an enormous mouth and butt whose constant efforts to diminish and emasculate Martin provide focus for his ire and jokes. It's interesting that comic barbs aimed at these women often involve equating them with animals—bears, dogs, and pigs. White people attempt to deny black men's humanity by reducing them to the status of animals; black men do the same to black women. Who is this female comedic construct? I've never met her. She is the result of the culture's racial hatred internalized by black men, and sometimes black women, as self-hatred and hatred of the closest other.

The truth is that black people are so committed to avoiding our collective history and desperate for the illusion of inclusion and affirmation that comes from reflection, however distorted, in popular culture, that we continue to consume these images, even when they make us uncomfortable. When I was growing up, the only television shows that featured black women were "Beulah," about a black maid, and "Amos 'n Andy," about a shiftless conniver. I wasn't allowed to watch them. My parents deemed Beulah, Kingfish, and his wife Sapphire unacceptable images for their children's consumption. As a teenager, there was Nichelle Nichols, who played Lieutenant Uhura on "Star Trek," but she existed in a distant galaxy, far from the immediacy of my daily need for reflection and affirmation. By the time my own daughter was born, the number of programs featuring black girls or women had increased, but often that simply meant additional stereotypes to navigate and discuss.

Because of the times and my politics, television was never the accepted, uncensored babysitter for my daughter that it is for many children today. As much as I could, I tried to be present when Misu watched television. If I was around, my daughter was unable to mindlessly and uncritically absorb "The Jeffersons," "Good Times," "What's Happening," "Benson," "Diff'rent Strokes," "The Facts of Life," or any of the other programs that starred black people. More than once, tired of my interjections and haranguing in the midst of her current favorite show, Misu would turn to me earnestly, open her eyes wide, and say plaintively, "Mom! Can we talk about what was wrong after 'The Jeffersons' goes off?" I was usually right there beside her, criticizing, and clarifying, emphasizing the dishonesty of the portrait of the po' but slap-happy family living in the projects on "Good Times," the racism inherent in the great white father raising two black sons on "Diff'rent Strokes," the irony that the smartest person in the governor's mansion was Benson, the black butler. It was crucial that I communicate to her that what she saw on television was not reality. It wasn't even, for the most part, black people's version of reality, but white people's rendering of what they imagined, or would like to believe, black people's reality to be. My point was the need to look at culture critically and for self-definition for black Americans, specifically for black women, assaulted as we are by loathing because of our gender, race, and history. It wasn't until "The Cosby Show" and "A Different World" came on television in 1983 and 1984 with fairly realistic portraits of hardworking, cross-class, non-pathological black people, that I felt I could relent somewhat in my efforts to critique and put into a broader context the images of us offered on television.

African Americans, the biggest consumers of television, are those who need it least and are most harmed by it. We have traded in our colored souls for a color TV. Television is the major way most of us get information. Despite the efforts of critics and activists, negative and often violent representations of black women, men, and children continue to dominate, with devastating effect. What would make us think we can watch television and then go into the real world with a positive image of, much less respect for, black women? Black People! Turn the television OFF!

Given black people's history in this country, most of us suffer from varying degrees of self-hatred. Most often black women internalize our self-hatred as our gender is conditioned to do, since nice girls don't get angry and self-hatred will definitely throw you into a rage. Instead, we decide that there is something wrong with us. That if we can just fix it, everything will be okay. We dye our hair blonde, stay on endless diets, deny our own needs, try to make ourselves simultaneously more passive, objectified, and visible and less actively threatening in the hope that "He" will choose us. Most often, the violence women do is to ourselves. Black men, as is men's conditioning, externalize their self-hatred, become angry, violent, cast it out onto each other, the community, onto us. Sometimes, in a definitive act of negation of black women, they turn to white women.

In her brilliant debut album, "Plantation Lullabies," composer/bassist/vocalist Me'Shell NdegéOcello has a song called "Soul on Ice":

We've been indoctrinated and convinced by the white racist standard of beauty   The overwhelming popularity of seeing, better off being, and looking white   My brothers attempt to defy the white man's law and his system of values   Defile his white women, but my, my,

Master's in the slave house again   Visions of her virginal
white beauty   Dancin' in your head   Your soul's on
ice   Your soul's on ice/Brother brother   Are you suffering from a social infection mis-direction   Excuse me
does the white woman go better with your Brooks
Brothers suit? I have psychotic dreams   Your jism in a
white chalk line   You let my sister go by/

The lyrics of NdegéOcello represent one of the few instances
in which a black woman calls out and critiques black men's fascination with white women and tries to put it in a historical-political
context. In general, black women know better than to publicly discuss the issue. It's as if by publicly acknowledging the phenomenon
and the pain it causes us we simultaneously identify ourselves as
emasculating bitches and assume responsibility for their choices:
See, he's with a white woman because those black women are just
too demanding, critical, sharp-tongued.

Though the discussion among black women may not often be
a public one, it is loud and clear in the company of women. Black
women voice feelings of betrayal, loss, rage, frustration, and self-
hatred/inferiority in their reactions to and efforts to understand
why, with an abundance of black women to choose from, black
men choose white women. The fact is that there are, at best, one
hundred black men for every 111 black women. When the number
of men who are unavailable because they are married, incarcerated,
drug/alcohol abusers, unemployable, or gay is factored in, that number is probably decreased by fifty percent. Then we've got to factor
in those who are simply not interested in black women, whose
souls, as NdegéOcello so powerfully puts it, turning the title of El-
dridge Cleaver's 1968 book on its head, are on ice.

The discussion about black men and white women is a discussion among black women: black men usually refuse to talk about it. When they do, their responses are disingenuous. The more cautious among them insist that it's not that they consciously "chose" a white woman, they "just fell in love." They conveniently cloak themselves in an adolescent notion of love as a state independent of history, politics, and cultural conditioning that we inadvertently and unintentionally "fall" into, like a sinkhole.

Given the historic and contemporary response of the dominant white culture to black men's interactions with white women, which include beating, castration, and lynching, and in the case of a black man jogging with a white woman in Utah several years ago, death by sniper fire, one is hard-pressed to accept black men's explanation that they simply "fell in love." As Jimi Hendrix asked, "Is this love, baby, or just confusion?"

Certainly the denigration of black women during and post-slavery and the simultaneous representation of white women as the ultimate and ultimately unattainable object of beauty is an important factor in black men's attraction to white women. So too is their simultaneous desire not only to be a part of the patriarchy but to undermine the patriarchal founding fathers. The civil rights movement, laws against segregation, the rescinding of laws against miscegenation, and the lip service paid to integration as an American ideal provided black men with increased access to white women.

A crucial factor is the way black women have been portrayed in the culture as figures of opposition to black men. The fact is that we were all oppressed by slavery. Black women's value was derived solely from being wombs that could produce additional slaves, free labor, and had nothing to do with our colluding with white men against black men. Yet, over time, it has become widely accepted in our communities that a significant degree of black men's oppression is black women's "fault." We have become the other, the enemy. Today, black women are told that we're "too aggressive," "judgmental," "taking the black man's jobs," and "getting over at the expense of black men." My favorite is "too successful," the ultimate oxymoron.

With all that separates us, most heterosexual black women want to love and be loved by a black man. But we are so trapped in bad history, negative representations, anger, and miscommunication that this becomes increasingly difficult. In addition, we refuse to face the facts of our situation: that available women far outnumber men, that sexual fidelity from men is largely a myth, and that we tacitly sanction informal and irresponsible polygamy, that most women will not marry and live happily ever after. Instead, we persist in believing in fairy tales. We compete with each other for men to the detriment of ourselves and building a sisterhood. We lie to ourselves and our daughters by holding out the obsolete carrot of the nuclear family. We yearn for an idealized, nonexistent notion of marriage, to the detriment of ourselves, black men, and black community. Times are so tough that almost any heterosexual black man with any job, single or married, is besieged by women and held to few if any standards of behavior and responsibility. We twist and reshape ourselves to appeal to men, accept stale crumbs and pretend they're cake, sacrifice ourselves on the altar of the Penis God, to ill effect.

Just as it is imperative that we begin to understand the forces that have shaped us and define who we want to be as black women, what our individual and collective agenda is, we must do the same when it comes to black men. Without standards, we will accept whatever comes down the road, simply project our fantasies and needs onto the men we meet and hope it takes. I have learned that other people, including men, are at best extra, not crucial, to happiness. Happiness is mine for the creating. I have learned that there is a difference between a man and a penis; the former is a rare thing, the latter can be easily found or bought at the sex toy store.

If the issue for black women is self-definition, part of that process involves telling men what we want from them. So for myself and all my sisters, the men I love, will love, and the ones I'll never know, I offer what I hope is a self-loving, free-thinking, political black woman's blueprint for what makes a man.

1. A man who likes himself.

    This may seem simplistic or obvious. It's not. A man must have goals and dreams for the future, but be comfortable with who he is in the present. This quality is often hard to find in black men, since we live in a culture that constantly degrades and denigrates blackness. Probably an implicit characteristic of a man who likes himself is that he has to be strong, otherwise how would he resist all the hatred coming at him?

2. A man who sincerely likes black women.

    This is definitely not the same thing as love. "Like" is the muscle that keeps people together when times are hard, the world is crashing in, and sex is boring. Black folks need to like each other, since the major signals we get from the dominant culture about ourselves are negative. A man should like and accept the qualities, sometimes contradictory, that make up women.

3. An honest man.

    Honest men are the ones you can trust, and in relationships honesty is the only policy. Lying is a form of manipulation and control, elements that guarantee an unhealthy relationship. If you're with someone you don't feel can deal with your truth, you shouldn't be with them. If you're lying because you don't want to be challenged, questioned, or pushed to grow, you should be in a relationship with a therapist.

4. A man who reads.

More than work-related manuals and the sports page of the newspaper. History, fiction, nonfiction, biography, poetry, it's all okay, as long as he reads, which indicates an interest in the world broader than "What do I need to know to do my job and male bond over sports?" It means he can bring knowledge and information into the relationship.

5. A man with a sense of humor.

My friend the writer Harry Allen describes humor as "the KY jelly of relationships. It lubricates everything else." A man should have the ability to laugh at the world, the people in it, and himself. Black people have traditionally used humor as a survival mechanism, the old "Laugh to keep from crying" strategy, and we need humor now as much as ever. It's also nice when that sense of humor is accented by a sense of the absurd.

6. A man who's working and self-supporting.

Most of the men I know have some experience they recount about a woman who they sincerely cared for who was a gold-digger, just looking for what he could do for her. The objective here is not a man who can pay a woman's bills, but one who can pay his own. Job description is not important. A sanitation worker, doctor, carpenter, lawyer, NBA star, or mailman is fine, as long as he lives decently, isn't in debt, and can split things fifty-fifty. The flip side of this is that black women need to let go of the "We-want-to-be-treated-just-like-we-think-white-women-are-treated" Cinderella complex and look for a man who can be an economic partner instead of a Mack Daddy.

7. A spiritual man.

Spirituality has nothing to do with organized religion, and you can be spiritual without having set foot in a house of worship in decades. A man should have a belief in some sort of higher power, and the interest in exploring it. That exploration can be done meditating, running, praying, making art, going to Narcotics Anonymous meetings, what's crucial is some belief, connection, and curiosity about a spiritual essence.

8. A sensual man.

This has as much to do with what goes on out of bed as in. A man should be affectionate, warm, physically accessible, and comfortable in his own body and yours. A truly sensuous man can create a hot spot in the middle of your kitchen that makes your stomach clench when you pass through it.

9. A man with progressive politics and a sense of history.

No self-hating, neo-conservative, "I got mine, don't worry 'bout his" men desired. A man should understand the need to transform this society into a humane one, and be willing to do some work toward that end.

10. A man with a tangible connection to family and community.

People who dislike their parents, siblings, other relatives, and have few friends usually don't make good partners. This is especially true if they don't like their mothers. A man should have a positive, adult relationship with his birth family and a connection to the larger community of black people. This connection can manifest through his job, volunteer work, political activism, or a casual, day-to-day involvement in the community in which he lives. Merely to be a member of the community of self is not enough.

11. A man who understands the linkage between racism and sexism.

   See Everyday Violence, Chapter 6.

12. A man who is available.

   This means a man who is able to be physically present, not one who promises to be there but doesn't show. Availability also means being introspective and expressive, a man who goes inside himself and thinks about what he finds there, then talks about it. Communication is a requisite for a relationship. A man should let a woman in on what he's thinking and feeling. When he does, women should listen.

THE DICKPOLITIK

QUEEN MOTHER MOORE, the grandmother of the cultural nationalist movement in what African American activists variously call Amerikkka, Babylon, and the Wilderness of North America, floats slowly toward the stage. It looks as though the men at her flanks lift her, it is as if she is gliding, and maybe she is, I cannot see her feet beneath the swirling fabric of her African robes. She is, as the nationalists say, an "Elder," which is a nice, Afrocentric way of saying old and wise. Light-skinned, loose flesh hangs in drapes underneath her smooth face, it is easy to see in the remaining hint of cheekbones and full lips that she was once a beautiful woman. Her eyes are darting, bright, quick, suggesting that her mind remains sharp. Once ascended she stands before us, looks out at the audience, clears her throat. I turn toward my friend Stanley Kinard, roll my eyes. He pats my hand in sympathetic warning. I hear him whisper, laughter in his voice, a giggle really, he is one of the few men I know who giggles, "Now, Jill. Wait. Don't go off."

I nod, acknowledging the pressure of Stanley's hand. We have been friends for a decade, a friendship that began with a shared concern for the black community and is regularly cemented by a tendency to laugh about the same things, corresponding world views, even similar tastes in food. Over the years we have attended dozens of meetings, rallies, and marches together, and this is not the first time we have seen or discussed Queen Mother Moore. Stanley knows that while I respect the sister and her long history in the movement, I also find her politics very male-centered, yet another example of acceptable black female leadership being those who ac-quiesce most enthusiastically to the peno-centric agenda of black men. Stanley knows me well enough to know that, eventually, I'm going to go off. He just doesn't want it to be here and now.

"I hear you all arguing about polygamy," the Queen Mother be-gins, her voice faint. "And you can talk about it as long as you want. But I'm here to tell you, men are like dogs!" Her voice grows stronger as she speaks, her throat gradually opening. I can hear her loud and clear now, she is almost growling. "A man's going to be sniffing around more than one woman, that's just how they are, like dogs," she continues passionately, voice quavering. "And there are not enough men for all of you women. You know that." She pauses, waiting for this hard fact to sink in, the messenger bearing black women yet more grim news. Her glance sweeps around the full auditorium. She waits for silence as she builds to the crescendo, keeps it short and sweet. The room is absolutely quiet.

"That's why polygamy is the answer!" she declares. In the au-dience, a few women nod their agreement. Others shake their heads quizzically, as if trying to expel a bothersome thought, suck their teeth, and roll their eyes, black women's body language for "Puh-leese, don't even start that shit." More than a few of the men nod smugly, applaud mildly, sit a little more righteously on their chairs—also known as thrones in the lingo of cultural nationalism—and why not? For most of them, polygamy is a two-fer, simultaneously satisfying their black nationalist yearning for a romanticized African past and their more contemporary American compulsion to get as much poontang as they can possibly handle. Or not handle, but think they can.

"Now, what I want, I want all you sisters who are in a polyga-mous relationship to stand up and tell your sisters what you have that they don't!" roars the Queen Mother.

It is a sweltering afternoon in the summer of 1979, and several hundred sweating black folks are crammed into the Brooklyn Ar-mory at the first convention of the Black United Front. The Front is a relatively new activist organization with chapters in a number of major cities that focuses on community organizing for social change and empowerment in the black community. The cavernous auditorium is populated predominantly by serious cultural nation-alists in full regalia. These are African Americans who dress in African fabric, collarless suits à la Tanzania's president, Julius Nyerere, prefer musk oil to Charlie!, do not straighten their hair, and gener-ally identify with African politics and customs more than they do anything that's going on in America. Many nationalists are also Pan-Africanists, and before it was safe or popular to evoke the name of Ghanian revolutionary Kwame Nkrumah or wear a "Free Nelson Mandela" T-shirt, they made up a core of black American activists involved in supporting movements for the independence of African nations and the end of the apartheid regime in South Africa. In the relative wasteland that is black political activism in the late 1970s, the nationalists are an important force. Unfortunately, in my experience, nationalists—with whom I have a lot in common and would have at one time defined myself—are usually weak on the gender issue. Kinda a "Me King, You Queen, Queen Obey King" take, if you know what I mean.

But by 1979, nationalism is one of the few options around for black people—particularly those in their twenties, as I am—looking to join a political-activist organization. We are the generation who grew up surrounded by numerous social movements, but by the time we came of age, most of them were defunct. Nationalism, we suspect, may be our last chance to participate in anything resembling the movements we grew up watching and yearning to participate in. By the late 1970s, the civil rights, Black Muslim, and Black Power movements have disappeared as the focus of activism. Gone are the beatings, hosings, and attacks by snarling German shepherds on black and white activists that brought the civil rights movement of the early 1960s into the living room of anyone who owned a television. The passage of the Voting Rights Act in 1965 and other major legislation has shifted the movement into the unsexy, non-telegenic courts, classrooms, and workplaces, as emphasis moved to enforcement of rights already—at least theoretically—won. The Black Muslim and Black Power movements, in the form of the Nation of Islam and the Black Panther Party, have been consumed by government-sponsored destabilization, internal dissension, and incarceration. All black movements for political change have been crippled by political assassinations, from Malcom X and Martin Luther King, Jr. in 1965 and 1968 to Fred Hampton and George Jackson in 1969 and 1971. In the end, specific political actions, rhetoric, or analysis doesn't seem to matter: a nonviolent, Christian, middle-class Martin King can have his head blown open just as easily as a Muslim radical advocate of self-defense like Malcolm X. The resounding and unavoidable message to black activists is clear: If you dare to seriously challenge the status quo, one of a number of forces in the culture will not hesitate to kill you.

The fragile coalition between black and white activists forged during the nonviolent sit-ins and Freedom Rides of the early 1960s and held together tenuously by mobilization against the war in Vietnam, has shattered. Those whites who weren't scared away from nonviolent activism by southern racists beat a hasty retreat in the face of the growing militancy and nationalism of black activists during the last years of the 1960s and the early 1970s. The end of the Vietnam War on April 29, 1975, when the United States military was driven from Vietnam by the victorious Vietcong, complete with televised images of macho employees of the greatest country on earth cowering on the roof of the U.S. embassy in Saigon and scrambling for a seat in a departing helicopter, was the official death knell of the organized movement. The war abroad having ended, many white people at home chose to ignore the wars in America. By the end of the decade, Black Nationalism offered one of the few refuges for black activists as yet unconvinced that the battle for civil rights and black power had irrevocably shifted, to quote Jesse Jackson, from the streets to the suites.

I grew up certain that the country I lived in was on the brink of enormous changes, that each day the world was different than it had been the day before, that the balance of power was shifting from the old, tired, and corrupt, embodied in Bull Connor, the war in Vietnam, Lyndon Johnson's defense secretary Robert McNamara, southern murders, lynchings, and bombings, to the youthful, energetic, and idealistic. We used to say don't trust anyone over thirty and mean it, as if we would never reach thirty ourselves. When I did, I was shocked, even though we had long since stopped saying that.

I became a teenager in 1965, made sixteen in 1968, turned

eighteen, the age of maturity, in 1970. But the rites of passage for earlier generations of middle-class girls, like having a sweet sixteen party, coming out and being introduced to society at a Cotillion Ball, pledging a sorority, going to college to meet and marry a nice doctor were, for many of my generation, obsolete. But as much as we had a clear sense of what we didn't want, we lacked a specific notion of what we did, what would replace those structures that we were rejecting. My parents, like many adults, seemed as confused as I was. Sometimes I even thought they were looking to us, the younger generation, for guidance. It was as if we were clearing the landscape for construction of something new and better, but without blueprints. The only thing to do was go with the flow. Two of the major streams that fed that flow were music and drugs. Often it seemed that Sly and the Family Stone, Jimi Hendrix, Cream, the Isley Brothers, and other musicians, aided by some wine, a joint, and a tab of acid or mescaline, were not only the best articulators of the hope and rage of that generation and that time, but that they had a plan, if I could only remember it once the high wore off. After the demise of the activism of the 60s and 70s, what was left was drugs and music; they became our lingua franca. We came of age on the cusp of something, on the verge of everything, the dawning of the Age of Aquarius, but by the time I'd turned eighteen in 1970, expectations had begun a downward slide. Reaching maturity between 1965 and 1970 was the equivalent of serving a five-year apprenticeship and having the factory close permanently on the day you became a journeyman. What was left were drugs and the music. If there were a television show about people my age in the 1970s, like "thirtysomething," it'd be called "Copping Something . . . and Then Listening to Music."

In 1976 I finish college and am searching for a place to practice the activism I came of age immersed in. I have some practical and many romantic notions about working for social change, about revolution, but no organizational structure in which to practice them. In college I have organized programs for International Women's Day, fought for open admissions and free tuition, written for the college newspaper, helped establish and worked with an organization that gets women into the overwhelmingly male and lucrative construction unions, supported the struggle for affirmative action and freedom in South Africa. When I get out of school I am ready to take on the real world, but the world into which I take my first steps as an adult is not the world I either prepared for or imagined.

As a teenager, I was attracted to the aggressive stance of Stokeley Carmichael, H. Rap Brown, and the Student Non-Violent Coordinating Committee's new militant strategy, prefer SNCC's in-your-face stance to the Christianity-based, appeal-to-the-dubious-moral-conscience-of-Americans approach of Martin Luther King, Jr. and the traditional civil rights organizations. Raised as an atheist or agnostic, I've never been sure which, my connection to organized religion, to preachers and the black church, was decidedly tenuous. I neither knew nor gave much thought to the existence of the traditional Christian notion of God. The world of black preachers, of which King was the finest representative, did not appeal to me. There was no way I could envision myself joining the ranks of dedicated church sisters delivering souls and smothered pork chop lunches to ministers wearing diamond pinkie rings, driving hogs, and preaching abstinence to the congregation while secretly sleeping with some needy sister in the choir. Worse was the notion of accepting hell on earth based on the promise of heaven in the hereafter. I'd been raised in a family that was into the here and now, that's when we wanted our just deserts; we'd deal with the afterlife if there was one, and if we got there. The rebellious, angry immediacy of black militance appealed to my teenage soul. These things, coupled with the fact that as the bloody 1960s ended and the 1970s commenced many civil rights and anti-war activists had lost faith in the efficacy of appealing to America on moral grounds, made the racially affirming and activist tenets of SNCC and the Black Panther Party in the latter days of the civil rights movement, and the cultural nationalism that later emerged, politically—and emotionally—appealing.

When Stokeley Carmichael terrifies America by simply daring to combine the words black and power, we cheer. It is as if the words combust into a call for violence, insurrection, revolution. With two words the brother from Trinidad becomes Nat Turner reincarnated one hundred years later, urging the slaves to revolt and visit swift and bloody retribution on their oppressors. We listen to Stokeley's words with rapt attention and to those of his successor, H. Rap Brown, who sums up our impatience with nonviolence when he says, "Violence is as American as apple pie." If the civil rights movement was based on the profound belief in both the power of appealing to Americans' moral center and the possibility of systemic transformation of American institutions, by the late 1970s cultural nationalism was an angry and cynical response to the perception that such transformation was, at best, severely limited, at worst impossible.

But the truth is that most of us who were teenagers in the late 1960s weren't going anywhere to be violent or nonviolent, except high school, where we knew it was best to behave generally and make the grade, or else our parents might get violent with us. I volunteered at the offices of Mobilization to End the War making phone calls and handing out leaflets, stuffed envelopes at SNCC headquarters, and raised money for SNCC when organizer Ralph Featherstone spoke at my high school. We listened, read, learned, soaked up the spirit of change from activists only a few years older than us, styling ourselves after them. It was not until some years later that I consciously realized that most of those in leadership, those I sought to emulate, were men, the women then, as now, largely invisible.

After school and on weekends we checked out the row of stores owned by the Nation of Islam on 116th Street in Harlem and went a few times to religious services at the mosque. But at fourteen and fifteen the separation of men and women rubbed me the wrong way, and the requirement that women cover their heads, arms, and legs was out of the question in the halcyon days of Afros, miniskirts, and free love. While I respected the members of the Nation of Islam, they were too strict, too stern, too straight, too damn scary to align with, a sentiment shared by most black people back then, quiet as it's now kept. A couple of times I visited the Black Panther Party headquarters in Central Harlem, where I was told that before I could have a black leather jacket, beret, and gun, which was what I really wanted, I must first prove my commitment by selling the Party's newspaper. I remember the men in the cramped office, dressed all in black, seemed much older than I was, incredibly intense, and vaguely threatening, the confluence of sex and revolutionary violence hung so thick around them I could smell it. I don't remember seeing any women around. Maybe they were in back, taking care of business. I took some papers, sold them the next day to my white friends at school, and never went back, although I continued to cheer the Panther's militancy from afar, contribute money to programs when asked, and read their newspaper regularly.

Most of my generation were, at best, part-time activists. We went to all the anti-war and civil rights demonstrations we could, often taking the bus to Washington. For us, Washington's monuments are not to presidents or institutions but demonstrations. When I pass the cold marble buildings that institutionalize government I can almost see the ghosts of hundreds of thousands of demonstrators, hear the roll of voices along the Tidal Basin in front of the Lincoln Memorial during the March on Washington in 1963. The spot in front of the Capitol where, during an anti-war demonstration, members of the wild Socialist Labor Party strung up and burnt an effigy of Nixon in a crowd of thousands of people, and when the wind blew we ran from burning cinders of Tricky Dick. The Supreme Court up on First Street where we marched in 1978 in support of affirmative action and against Alan Bakke's suit alleging reverse discrimination because he didn't get into medical school at the University of California at Davis. The mall where hundreds of thousands protested Nixon's bombing of Cambodia the winter of 1969.

Three decades later, many of us who are children of the 1960s have remained in a strange limbo, straddling two worlds, the one we have and the one we wanted. A few of us have remained focused, committed idealists. In the process of earning a living, some of us try to do work that in some way speaks to our values, not the so-called "Family Values" of the religious right, which really are not values at all but an attempt to resuscitate the Dying White Male Culture at the expense of colored people, women, gay people, and our children. We try in some way to live and work in ways that create a more equitable, humane America, or at least not make it a worse place than it has become. We try to forget the 1960s because it's just too painful. We endeavor not to think about those years, talk about them, avoid feeling them. But there must be a 1960s gene, it's in our molecular memory, because our children intuit, ask questions, want to know, even in the face of our collective denial.

It is on our children that this collective denial has had its most profound and devastating impact. They are young people who came of age in the 1980s, their world defined by Ronald Reagan and George Bush, the rise of the right wing, the deconstruction of social programs, the growth of neo-conservatism and the "Christian" right, the radical shrinking of the economy. The most well adjusted of them are still confused, at a loss, cynical. The worst enraged, despairing, and violent. Their daily experience lets them know in no uncertain terms that there is something very wrong with our society, but they are without models for creating alternatives, have no tools, no movement. They mistake the music of hip hop for a movement, which it is not. Rap may articulate real conditions and sentiments in some communities, but stating the problem is not the same as building a movement. That requires organization, strategy, and an agenda, something that is missing in young people's lives. Much of the responsibility for this is due to the silence of my generation, their parents. We do not talk about what we did during the 1960s and 70s, where we were, how it felt to be alive and committed then, how, why, and when we screwed up, the things that happened politically and personally to make us lose that belief in the possibility of change, in activism. I think we are silent because we are heartbroken, have not figured out how to tell young people what happened without transferring onto them our own feeling of hopelessness and despair. With our silence we allow the right wing to negatively define the period, to dismiss or ignore the amazing confluence of a number of movements all committed to creating a truly inclusive America that occurred in the 1960s, and instead define the period by bell bottoms, drugs, tie-dyed clothing, and rock music, all style and no substance. It's like a bad psychedelic painting by Peter Max: in such a stoned, cartoon character world, could we be anything but tripped-out dreamers? As a generation, we need to get over it, take voice, tell the children the truth. That those decades were reshaped by ordinary people doing extraordinary things, the everyday people that most of us are. There was a revolution toward the left in the 1960s and early 1970s, the movement shifted right in the 1980s and 1990s. It is up to us to decide what direction we go in at the millennium.

But in the last half of the 1970s, the black nationalist movement, like whiteness, or the retreat to the safety of the middle class, or drugs, or further marginalization, or mainstream "gimme a piece of the boys' pie" white feminism, was a xenophobic reaction to the political and psychic devastation that ended the revolution of the 1960s, part of the death throes that went on for a decade, ended with the crowning of Ronald Reagan in 1980.

For me, the stakes are high at the meeting of the Black United Front in 1979. It is either the last chance at resuscitation of whatever is left of the political passion of the 1960s and 1970s or the final gasp of the nationalist movement. The Brooklyn Armory is so crowded that Stanley and I have to respectfully push our way through hordes of people to get into the main auditorium. On the way, we pass dozens of vendor tables piled high with books, oils, incense, art, African hats and clothing, ease through the aroma of peas and rice, curry, mixed vegetables, and fish. Stanley and I are, as the most popular chant of the day goes, "Fired Up! Can't Take No More!," looking, as we have together for many years, for an organization to connect with. The old, elected leadership is more concerned with getting reelected, making political hay, and getting paid than they are with a failed education system, high unemployment, the reign of heroin and crime, the health care crisis, police violence, or any of the other issues affecting those of us who actually live in a black community.

The auditorium is filled with people who have participated in and survived a number of political movements, all there in search of refocus, rejuvenation, leadership. Most come from a black nationalist base, believe that a movement can be formed based upon the idea that within the United States black Americans are a distinct nation, and that the political, economic, and cultural needs of that black nation are of paramount importance. Nationalism, our withdrawal into a proscribed community defined by racial identification and solidarity, is the black-hand side of white people's post-1960s retreat into whiteness. It is a visual as well as a political separation. Many of those present wear clothes made of African fabric, dashikis, the small caps called kufis on their heads. Dreadlocks abound. The women are similarly dressed in African prints, many wear gelees (African fabric wrapped around the head in fantastic and beautiful shapes) or Muslim-inspired veils. There are few bare arms, legs, or glimpses of cleavage present, since one of the tenets of the nationalist movement is that women should, if not exactly cover themselves, dress demurely, and in fact a few women in the room look like they're in purdah, the seclusion of women practiced by some Muslims and Hindus, covered in dark clothing head to toe, including a veil over their noses and mouths, with only their eyes showing. I think that must be torture, especially in summertime, breathing hot, funky air through a layer of cloth. I draw a line at being told by nationalists, fashion mavens, or anyone else what to put on my body. I hardly wear high heels anymore, even though I grew up with a mother with pretty legs who wore them every day and taught my sister and I that, having inherited her good legs, it was our obligation to wear heels and show them off to our best advantage. Experience taught me that too often what high heels do is get you screwed, literally or figuratively, not to mention a bad back and gnarled feet. I have learned the two most important things for women when it comes to shoes is that they be comfortable and good for running.

Even though the meeting begins with speakers talking about building a Black United Front that will address issues of police violence, the deterioration of black communities, how to organize and mobilize the people, the discussion turns, as it all too frequently does during the heyday of cultural nationalism, to polygamy. When I look up polygamy in the dictionary the definition reads, "marriage in which the spouse of either sex may have more than one mate at the same time," but nationalists never mention the option of women having more than one husband, the discussion is always framed in terms of a man having many wives. There's a lot of talk about the African and Islamic roots of polygamy, the ways in which a polygamous environment positively supports the community, the sacrifices the serious African man who chooses polygamy is required to make, but as far as I'm concerned, this is simply an effort to find historical justification for something that, in twentieth-century America, is problematic at best. With few exceptions, polygamy as practiced in African America, or at least in Harlem and Brooklyn, boils down to nothing deeper than legitimized fucking around, except you can do it at home. When it comes to polygamy in African America, we're not talking about a man assuming responsibility for his diseased brother's older, maybe unattractive wife and too many, out-of-control children out of a sense of economic and social duty. In America, polygamy is a semi-legitimate way to have a younger, flyer woman without your older, long-suffering wife justifiably going off or heading for divorce court. Polygamy is an explosive topic in the black community, and at its mention voices are raised, people get loud, polygamy has divided those in the armory into those who are pro, those who are con, and many, most of them women, who are silent. Or have been silenced.

In general, the men support the option of polygamy, the most vocal women do not. The meeting is on the verge of deteriorating into screaming argument when suddenly it's quiet. I look to see what brought on the silence, since it's not often you find yourself surrounded by silent black people. Black folks damn near always have something to say, even when we're just talking shit, we are big into verbal improvisation. Black comedians from Moms Mabley to Redd Foxx to Richard Pryor know and use this, some of their best material comes from the spontaneous combustion between them and their audience.

I look around to see what brought about this unlikely silence, and that's when the Queen floats onto the scene. As far as I can discern her appearance is impromptu, necessitated by the dissension created by the mention of polygamy. The Queen commands the room. It is as if some ancient elder from our collective, glorious African past has materialized in the Brooklyn Armory to lay down the law. We all know it is time to shut up and listen. But do we have to obey?

When Queen Mother concludes her brief sermon with the words, "That's why polygamy is the answer!" standing on stage looking out at a sea of attentive faces, the expression on her face is one of challenge. The room erupts in applause, ululation, cheers, a few boos. The amazing thing is that when the Queen Mother calls on the women in polygamous marriages to "stand up and tell these other sisters what you have that they don't!" that sweltering afternoon, women actually stand. They rise from their chairs and glare proudly ahead, a few with babies riding on their hips, soldierettes in the army of polygamy, charter members of the brave new polygamous vanguard. It's not unlike that moment in a church service when the minister asks, "Who is ready to welcome Christ into their lives?" except we're not talking about Christ but a mortal man, and while Christ might want to get into our lives, the brothers are more interested in the boudoir. Looking at the women who stand up, I cannot help notice that they are very young. I wonder where they'll be in five years. I am not optimistic. That's when I turn toward Stanley again, moan, "Oh, God, Stan." I know he hears me, because the pressure of his hand on my arm tightens, I can see the tics that are the beginning of a giggle around the corner of his mouth, but he stares straight ahead, does not answer. Maybe silence from this opinionated, talkative, sometimes argumentative man is answer enough, and in a way, it doesn't matter, because there's nothing to say. At that moment in the armory, under the gaze of Queen Mother Moore, surrounded by a sea of nationalists, promojites, and the polygamous vanguard, it's over. I'm gone. Politically, psychically, and emotionally outta here, I couldn't tell you another word that is said, probably didn't even hear them over the rush of rage, disgust, and blood roaring in my head.

The surprise appearance of Queen Mother Moore as the iconographic nationalist woman, hauled out to explain to manless women what we're missing, highlight the advantages of polygamy, and at the same time silence and isolate the naysaying black women in the room, is like some nationalist sleight of hand in a bad magic show, and I'm not going for it. It's father knows best all over again, except on a larger scale: Now you see her! Now you don't! Women should be seen but not heard, should not speak until spoken to. This meeting is not, I abruptly understand, about partnership and power, but about patriarchy and pussy, and I cannot participate. "Stanley!" I wail softly, almost keening, a lamentation for the death of my last hopes for nationalism. "Be cool," he whispers without a hint of laughter in his voice. "Be cool."

Stanley and I have remained friends and political allies through the years, united by a respect and affection for each other, but perhaps most of all by an ongoing search for a politic and activism that will move black people and America forward. Stanley has addressed this need by working in a variety of political campaigns, community-based organizations, aligning himself with a number of movements, and finally forming an organization of his own in Brownsville, Brooklyn, the Carter G. Woodson Cultural Literacy

Project, which works with students. I've been working as a journalist, moved in and out of political organizations, tried to make change where and when I could. For twenty years we have talked regularly. Periodically, we talk about polygamy. This sometimes comes up in the context of my critiquing men, Stanley critiquing women, or both of us critiquing the dismal state of relations between the sexes, and how that affects and distorts the whole idea of family and responsibility among black people. I no longer froth at the mouth, begin raving, or have blood rush to my ears when the subject comes up. Intellectually speaking, I can see the theoretical merits in polygamy, but practically, I can't imagine a way to make it work in this society, with these damaged African Americans. We are still looking for positive ways to impact upon a black community that, nearly two decades later, is fragmented by the effects of racism and self-hatred in its many guises: unemployment, poverty, crime, drugs, illiteracy. Much as we hoped it was, nationalism, especially for black women, wasn't part of the solution, but part of the problem.

Black women have always been the backbone of community organizations, churches, and political movements, gotten little or none of the credit, and stood demurely behind the male preacher/politico/activist while he pontificated at the press conference. But we also have a long history of independence and self-determination. Strong, independent, black women have always been fixtures in black political movements, although usually not in leadership. Women were not strangers to the political movements of the 1960s and 70s, though oftentimes the dickpolitik of these movements made these women virtually invisible. Civil rights activists Ella Baker and Fannie Lou Hamer are examples of sisters who were driving forces as activists and strategists, but virtually unknown to the public and largely unheralded until their deaths. Given black women's history of activism, a primary task of nationalism, conscious or subconscious, was to develop a strategy that would keep women doing the bulk of the day-to-day, behind-the-scenes work while remaining subservient to black men. The alternative was not only the loss of women's labor, work so crucial that the writer Zora Neale Hurston has described black women as "the mules of the world," but the continuing and expanded development of women in leadership roles, a situation that was anathema to the patriarchal, nationalist credo.

For black women, nationalism was made into the alternative to feminism. Black men couldn't simply dismiss black women's participation in movements for social change as irrelevant; that would have been ineffective and self-destructive. After all, this was a generation of women who had grown up and had their values formed by the civil rights and anti-war movements. Therefore, it was important psychologically, politically, and practically both to include black women and to find an alternative to the expanding feminist movement, something that would keep us in gender check and still doing the work.

The black nationalist movement, in spite of its romanticized rhetoric about black women, was essentially anti-female, and attempted to relegate gender issues, once again and once and for all, to the very back of African America's political bus. Couched in the mythical legitimacy of some pseudo-African history in which all men were powerful Kings, most women powerless but adored Queens, and polygamy ruled the land, nationalism at its worst used bad history to justify the continued subordination of black women. According to the nationalist construct, every African American had been a king, queen, or held some other exhalted status in the glorious Africa of yesteryear. You never heard anyone identify themselves as a peasant or farmer. It makes one wonder who was doing the work. The seductive aspect of the black nationalist movement was that its rhetoric appeared to exalt and celebrate black women, to reverse erasure, make us visible, when in fact it was more about a uniform change, a little cosmetic makeover, brand-new packaging wrapped around the same old same old. Liberation, we were told, demanded that we shake off the shackles of European and American culture, get back in touch with our true, African selves. No more fried or relaxed hair for us, Afros and dreads were the thing. The true African Queen, in some strange crossbreeding of black nationalism, Islam, and Puritanism, wore long dresses, long sleeves, and headwraps, sometimes even a modified veil, eased through the world demurely, righteously, barely visible, mouth most definitely shut, like the memory of words that remain on the page after the eraser has done its work. It was a world that existed after men, rarely beside them, never in front of them, except as an Afrocentric stencil on a politically correct T-shirt. A central tenet of the black nationalist movement was black men creating a patriarchy of their very own, and as in all patriarchies, it is the women who lost out.

Black nationalists, with the acquiescence and sometimes assistance of a racist, uninformed, and disinterested white culture that as often as not neither saw black women nor cared what we felt, presented the problems and demands of white women and black women as polar opposites. Nationalists and black men in general dismissed discrimination and oppression based on gender as an evil construct of spoiled, ungrateful, complaining, grasping white women who, having benefited since slavery days from the labor of black women and men, now wanted to abdicate the throne onto which white men and slave labor had placed them. Black women, exploited, oppressed, overworked beasts of burden, were the ones who had put the white woman where she no longer wanted to be. It would be folly, we were told, to join her in any part of her exodus. Instead, we should simply watch, be wary, and wait. Our time on the throne was near at hand, our nationalist brothers told us, as long as we obeyed the dickpolitik and followed the leader. While the dominant white male patriarchy attempted to discredit the feminist movement, characterizing its leaders as shrill, ungrateful, demanding, bra-burning wenches, nationalist black men, themselves patriarchal aspirants, echoed the same sentiments. But while white males condemned feminism without immediately offering up a pacifying alternative, black men did. Forget feminism, they told us. The antidote to being Mammy wasn't to support the political, economic, and social equality of women (the simple definition of feminism), it was to become a black nationalist, be a Queen! We would no longer have to serve Miss Ann, but, if we played our cards right, could become her. Nationalists essentially colluded with white men and mainstream media to portray feminism and the feminist movement as antithetical to black women who, unlike these crazy white women, had never had it good, loved men, weren't dykes, and liked wearing a bra. Feminism was, as many nationalist brothers told me during the 1970s, "a white girl's thing, because our problem is racism." Twenty years later racism is alive and very well, there is no national voice or organization fighting for the rights of black women, and most of us are far from being Miss Ann, although more black men, many of them lapsed nationalists, are busy balling her.

If white women were tired of being Miss Ann, put on a pedestal to go mad or under a bell jar to dry up, black women were told we no longer had to be Mammy, waitin' on Miss Ann. Now we could be Miss Ann, take the place white women were deserting. When white women protested that child bearing and raising was not inherently fulfilling for many women and demanded entry into a lucrative and powerful workplace, black women, historically forced to be working mothers, were told that to be a full-time babymaker and housewife were wonderful, rewarding roles. Both women and men were responding to the new control that came to women via the introduction in 1960 of birth control pills and the legalization of abortion in 1973. The inclination of most women was to embrace, celebrate, and use the new freedoms the pill and abortion offered. The response of men was to attempt to reassert the power of the patriarchy over women's sexuality and reproductive organs. Black nationalist men did this through the assertion that both birth control and abortion were just another diabolical example of genocide. Black women who chose to exert control over their reproductive systems were seen as aiding and abetting this evil program of racial extinction.

"You're like a brown rubber doll men buy to masturbate with" is what Byrd told me in early 1975. I was twenty-two and trying to return to college, and Misu had just turned two when I decided to abort an unwanted pregnancy. "The only reason to have sex is for procreation," he told me coldly, turned his back, and went to sleep. This was news to me, since for most of the years we'd been together I'd steadily used birth control and we'd had an active sex life. But I'd also been younger, dumber, less focused. The birth of Misu and the often overwhelming demands of motherhood, coupled with my being accused of child abuse in 1974, made it clear to me how vulnerable I was, how ill-equipped to provide for and protect myself, much less my little daughter. That I lived in a historical moment when I could choose to postpone motherhood to pursue an education seemed wonderful to me; the man I was living with did not see it that way. What were liberating choices for me were to him negative, anti-family, anti-male, and anti-nationalist. Rather than view my independence and determination as a compliment to him, it was a threat, the ultimate turn-off.

The "sex is for procreation" line was about ego, control, male dominance. As long as he controlled my reproductive organs I was a sensuous, loving earth mother. When I took control of my own body I became hostile, desexualized, unattractive. I do not think my husband was denying himself my physical charms to make a point. I spent the final months we were together looking for signs of this, attempting to coax him into non-procreative sexual relations, with little success. I truly believe my decision to abort, return to school, and use birth control was a near absolute sexual turn-off. If he could not control my body, he no longer wanted me. I left him in late 1975.

This notion that black women's independence is a contributing factor to black male oppression has long been a powerful subtext in the black community and its political, cultural, and social movements. It is founded on the belief that women inherently have it easier, that we are less threatening and therefore given more leeway by the dominant white culture. As a result, one of the requirements of black women in organizations, from the slave church to early political campaigns to the civil rights movement, has been that we push black men forward while ourselves stepping back, even when we are equally or more capable of leadership. The black nationalist movement was no exception. Far too much time and energy was spent on quasi-Afrocentric posturing, bullshit pomp and circumstance legitimized by rhetoric, clothing, and phony historical justifications for what in the end boiled down to plain old bad behavior. Women were visible and factored into black nationalist politics to the degree that we functioned as supporters of men. The possible manifestations of that support were, as always, severely proscribed. Nationalism required that we do the behind-the-scenes work, keep our mouths shut in public, and in private happily assume the prone position at the whim of our king, the better to produce more—male—warriors. Nothing really changed for black women except the rap and the costumes.

No longer was an unemployed man who refused to look for work and appeared content to live off the meager earnings of his woman what my mother would have called a "lazy bum." The nationalist movement turned him into a Black King, one of former head of black studies at City College of New York (my alma mater) and Afrocentric ideologue Leonard Jeffries' "Sun People," meaning black people who originally came from warm climates, as opposed to "Ice People," Europeans who came from colder climes. Men who refused to buy into the white man's system by working as a slave, but seemed to have little problem with his woman's enslavement, since it was "easier" for black women, benefiting from the largesse of "her natural ally, the white man," were to be respected and supported. By black women. If you thought your man was an adulterous, unfaithful dog in the nationalist era, think again. He was an African King expanding his wealth through the production of children, a man's greatest resource, and in the process taking care of the legitimate sexual and social needs of the sisters.

In spite of its abuses and ruses and the overwhelmingly negative impact on black women and relationships between black women and men, black nationalism also had some positive impact. The most important and lasting effect of the nationalist movement is the ways in which it promoted and popularized the study of Africa, African Americans, and the Diaspora. Popular interest in African history, art, culture, literature, politics, and religion was spurred by the nationalist movement, as was the interest in African and African American studies and the concept of Afrocentricism. This knowledge was crucial to the creation of a new, positive, and historically grounded sense of self among African Americans. Certainly the institutionalization of black and African studies on college campuses is a direct result of the nationalist movement.

But in the dismal 1970s, these positive outgrowths were still in formation, it was the symbols and rhetoric of black nationalism that seduced. Naive as it seems today, there really was a time when I believed that physical symbols reflected political consciousness, when wearing an Afro or dreadlocks or cornrows was more often than not an indication of political perspective, not simply the currently hip style, easily dispensed with and straightened out when the fashion changed. Even if you'd never been to Africa, when a woman wound a length of fabric around her hair, it was with some sense of an African connection in her heart, it was an affirmative act, not simply another way to be fly or cover up what we hipply call in the 90s "a bad hair day," forgetting that for most of our tenure here in America, the dominant culture has defined damn near all black people's hair days as bad. The flowing robes, nose rings, multiple earrings, kente cloth, and dashikis were symbolic declarations of a nationalist independence that spoke for us before we opened our mouths. At their best, these symbols spoke of self-love, a new aesthetic, thoughtful introspection, of positive self-definition in a culture whose few definitions of us were invariably negative.

Early on, the nationalist movement seemed affirmative, an answer to the ongoing search for positive identity, some protection against the overwhelming negativity, and possibly a place of visibility and voice for black women. Nationalism offered an ideology, a sense of history and culture, a political agenda—it even told us how to look and what to wear. While I did not completely swallow the line that my only problem was racism, like many women in the 1970s I put most of my gender issues on the back burner. I was in my twenties, the mother of a toddler, and certainly not oblivious to the nationalist line. I was seduced by the rhetoric and style of black nationalism, the notion that in embracing an African past I could find affirmation, self-love, identity, the political tools to transform the future. This is not to say that the signs that nationalism was oppressive to women weren't there, they were, I just didn't know how to interpret them. It was some years before it became completely, irrevocably clear to me that trying to determine whether the discrimination I experience from white people is a result of sexism or racism is most often a waste of time. Who cares? When it comes to black men, there's no question: it's about gender. Whatever the reason, and whoever's doing the discriminating, it's wrong.

Twenty years later, it is clear that not forcing the black nationalist movement to deal with its own patriarchy and chauvinism was a fatal mistake. The continuing erasure of black women as an important constituency, concern, or voice in the debate, both in and outside the black community, is evidence enough of that. Looking back with always 20-20 hindsight, black women would have been better served by confronting the nationalist movement and forcing it to deal not only with its sexism but with issues specifically affecting black women. If we had, it is possible that not only would nationalism have survived and evolved into a relevant and viable movement, but at the very least some of the problems internal to the black community—the proliferation of households headed by poor women, violence against women, and the alienation of fatherless black male and female children—would have been, if not alleviated, at least eased. Barring that, sisters should have jumped feet first into the feminist movement and used our transformative powers to make it address our needs and concerns. Instead, we put our issues on the back burner, all our eggs in the nationalist basket, and our needs second. In many ways what black nationalism did was create a pseudo-historic, Afrocentric context for patriarchy. As much as nationalists disdained the white women's feminist movement as just a bunch of spoiled, middle-class women trying to get a piece of white men's pie, they were simultaneously deeply committed to cutting themselves a wedge of the patriarchy, at our expense.

Twenty years after the heyday of the black nationalist movement, a few black women may still be waiting for the King to address us and our concerns, but most of us have given up. We are in limbo, with an attitude. Many black men seem absolutely unconcerned about us, a stance they rationalize, if challenged, by declaring that black women have it easier, have "made it," and presumably no longer have any problems. Some seem as if they plain don't like or want to be bothered by us. Some don't even see us.

The black nationalist movement was probably the last American political movement in which the public participation of black women was essential, if only to do the scut work and play the roles of polygamous Queen, bearer of babies, and woman in need of protection by the King. Our alternative, we were told, was to aid in the emasculation and destruction of the black male, to collude with our archenemy, Senator Daniel Patrick Moynihan, author of the 1965 study "The Negro Family: The Case for National Action." Otherwise known as the Moynihan Report, the document took a hard look at statistics relating to the black family and reached the conclusion that it was in dire straits. One of the points Moynihan made was the rapid and, as he viewed it, disturbing increase in households headed by black women. He wrote, "In essence, the Negro community has been forced into a matriarchal structure which, because it is so out of line with the rest of the American society, seriously retards the progress of the group as a whole, and imposes a crushing burden on the Negro male and, in consequence, on a great many Negro women as well." The assumption was that matriarchy, or simply women in leadership, was inherently wrong. On that both the Kings and the senator agreed. Back then, the worst thing a black woman could do was be a black matriarch. Better, as a nationalist brother said in the 1970s, for black women to refuse work if it meant being the sole support of the family, than to "help the white man cut the black man's dick off." And what, pray tell, about the black children, what would they eat? "If the children have to die for the black man's manhood, so be it" was his smug response. I later found out that he lived in Brooklyn, had two wives, several children, and didn't work: his wives and children received welfare. I looked for him at nationalist-type gatherings for a while, eager to confront him with my knowledge, to have him explain to me how being unemployed and dependent upon the state was penis affirming. I never saw him again, but occasionally I wonder what happened, not to him, but to those wives and babies.

The major accomplishment of the black nationalist movement was the relegation of the interests and needs of black women—for work, education, health care, physical safety, self-determination, in short, a voice in the discussion of political, economic, and social issues—to not only secondary, but more dangerously, irrelevant status. Nationalism created a false dichotomy, one that prevails twenty years later, which suggests that for a black woman to be self-interested, to be a feminist, is not only an oxymoron, but treachery, akin to holding the King's penis while the white Devil cuts it off. Couched in a patina of bad history, righteousness, quasi-benevolence, and a sincere yearning for a romantic, idealized African "past," nationalism evoked either a nonexistent or unpleasant African past in which men were men, women were their chattel, and everyone was happy. It was black male sexism, plain and simple. The effect of black male sexism and the nationalist movement on black women was like smoke: you could smell it, often see it, and sometimes feel it, but you couldn't grab it, get ahold of it. Nationalist attitudes toward black women and feminism were personal, subjective, social, and psychological. Black women who broached the subject of the treatment of women—usually avoiding the word feminism, since we all knew it would set the brothers off—were dismissed as misguided, white-identified, assimilated, treacherous, horny, and, if all that failed to shut them up, the worst of all possible uncontrollable women, lesbians. The simple mention of gender issues, much less declaring ourselves feminist, most often resulted in our being not only tossed unceremoniously out of the race, but also desexualized. The price of being a black feminist was both our race and gender. We were, effectively, erased.

That day at the Brooklyn Armory is an important one for me, the final step in the realization that I do not belong in the nationalist movement, that at the moment there is no place a vocal, self-loving, arrogant black woman can call her political home. The irony is that even though I have not yet publicly defined myself as a feminist because I know it will make the men crazy, don't want to be cast out of the race because I have no place to go, and am still hoping maybe the movement will accommodate my feminist leanings if I just don't use the "F" word, my silence didn't work. The identity nationalism offered me as idealized "Queen" left me as powerless and voiceless as always. There was a brief window when the nationalist community could have challenged itself on its sexism, chauvinism, and patriarchy, but it was a moment willfully ignored, as it turns out, for the short-term thrill of a few brothers being able to strut around chanting, "Oh yes, it's good to be the King." The scene at the Armory and a demonstration a few months earlier are the seminal events in my letting go.

In August 1979, the parents of a young, mentally ill Brooklyn man, Luis Baez, called the police for help when he became unruly. When the police arrived, Baez pulled a pair of scissors. Supposedly fearing for their lives, five cops circled him and shot him twenty-four times. (In November, as is usual in police shootings, a Brooklyn grand jury found no criminal liability.) Not long after Baez' murder, Stanley Kinard and I go together to a march to and demonstration in front of Brooklyn's 77th Precinct, where the cops who killed Baez are stationed. The demonstration is led by Reverend Herbert Daughtry, head of New York's Black United Front; there are several hundred people present. So there we are, marching toward the precinct, chanting, "Fired Up! Can't Take No More!" when the police, parked along the route of the march in patrol cars and accompanying us on horseback, suddenly attack. They run toward us, throw bottles at the demonstrators, shout and curse, guns drawn. A police car even begins to drive, and not slowly, into the crowd. Without warning or provocation, what had been an impassioned but peaceful demonstration turns into a police riot. People are screaming, running, scattering, panicked, their faces, and I'm sure mine, look totally shocked, although why should we have been, since we are demonstrating against cops who'd pumped twenty-four bullets into a mentally disturbed person armed with a "lethal" pair of scissors.

Stanley and I look for Reverend Daughtry and the march's other leaders, but they are nowhere to be found. The cops advance, bottles crashing around us. Stanley grabs my hand and we start running too. As is so often true in America we're more certain what we're running from than what we're running toward. We dart into a side street to catch our breath, figure out where to go, lean against the brick wall of a tenement, panting. "Where's Reverend Herbie? Where's Reverend Herbie? What's the plan? Where's the leadership?" I say, looking round.

We stay there for many long minutes. People run by us howling, bleeding, bottles shatter, the police advance. Reverend Herbie does not circle the block, reappear, jump out to lead us to the mountaintop, or at least out of the war zone. Neither Reverend Daughtry nor any of our other leaders come around. We are left hanging, to fend for ourselves. Stanley and I make our way safely from the police riot. Hopefully, we walk by Daughtry's church, the House of the Lord Pentecostal Church on Atlantic Avenue, hoping to find sanctuary, but the doors are closed, the windows dark.

It is not many months later that Stanley and I sit together at the Brooklyn Armory, my last dance with the black nationalist movement. I feel heartbroken, as if I've been in a relationship in which I've invested everything I had and woken up one morning to find the whole shebang looted by my partner, only worse, since my connection to and need for a mass movement is larger than any yearning for a man I've ever had. I know the saying "When the going gets tough, the tough get going" is supposed to mean the tough rise to the challenge, but in my experience what it most often boils down to is "When the going gets tough, the tough run." It is on that night that I face the reality that the 1960s are truly over, that we have no movement, no strategy, no leadership—as we step into 1980 and the reign of King Ronnie—to deal with black men's dickpolitiks or a police precinct on the rampage, much less the transformation of America.

By 1980 I turn inward, away from organized activism, into myself and my computer. Much as I hate to recognize and admit it, I put my dreams of the 1960s and 70s on the back burner and join the female, politically progressive, colored version of "The Me Generation." I wage my war with words, but it is really not enough. Occasionally I venture out into professional organizations, union activism, corporate infiltration, but most often wind up disillusioned and beating a hasty retreat.

The tragedy is that most of us, black women and men, are worse off now than we were twenty years ago. Yet as a people we still refuse to acknowledge and deal with issues of gender and the need to battle racism and sexism simultaneously. Black men cling to the redemptive potential of a more benevolent patriarchy. Too many black women continue to believe both that it's all about race and that the men are inherently more important. In such positions, dialogue, unity, and creative action are truly impossible. Women and men remain at once purveyors and victims of the dickpolitik.

In the late 1980s, it became chic to refer to black men as an "endangered species," a term that at first seemed inappropriate. It is usually applied to animals in the wild in need of government protection, not human beings in urban America who, as often as not, need to be protected from the government and, increasingly, each other. Over time, the ways in which the term "endangered species" accurately sums up contemporary America's view of black men as something less than human, simultaneously endangered, dangerous, and animalistic, has become clear to me. The sentiment that people of African descent are not quite human has historically been used to vindicate our ill treatment, starting with the Christian justification of slavery as necessary to civilize the "heathen savages." Black leaders quickly embraced the phrase, as if declaring the likelihood of their extinction might elicit some positive response from the government agencies, elected officials, and gun manufacturers gleefully helping it along. It didn't. Cuts and attacks continue unabated even as journalists, pundits, legislators, and others, a few of whom might be sincere, bemoan the awful state of affairs.

As for black women, we're never mentioned as endangered and rarely as anything else. Most of the time it's as if we don't exist, even though we're the ones who birth, nurture, and raise the black male children who grow to endangered species-hood. Because of our failure to create a viable black women's movement, black women are invisible and voiceless. Whether you were disturbed by the implication of black men's impending extinction—and I was—or greeted the prospect happily, eager to do your part for the cause of no more Negroes with penises, the focus on black men as an endangered species excluded black women from the dialogue. The message in this exclusion was that the problems, interests, and agendas of black men had no fundamental connection to or effect on black women, who presumably had no problems, or at least none worth talking about. Almost at the millennium, our current situation is worse than the oppressive and lowly status we were accorded in the civil rights and black nationalist movements; nowadays we have no status whatsoever. Black men have at least been declared endangered, which suggests someone considers them worth saving. For the most part, when it comes to critical internal or external issues in the culture, black women simply don't exist.

EVERYDAY VIOLENCE

Until I was thirty-two years old and my then-husband hit me upside my head so hard he punctured my eardrum, I thought I wasn't the type of woman who got hit. I wasn't clear exactly what type of women men did hit, I only knew I wasn't the type.

My mother always told my sister and me, "If a man hits you, leave. Because if he hits you once and you stay, he'll hit you again, harder." This was one of the few times I immediately took my mother's advice to heart, not being able to figure how this admonition was a ploy on her part to deprive me of some wicked pleasure. Then I took it one step further, decided to become the type of woman a man wouldn't dare hit. Since there were few role models for black women out there, and because when I was growing up women didn't talk publicly or loudly about getting their ass whipped, I wasn't quite sure how to do this. I knew that men sometimes beat women from scraps of overheard conversation, from occasionally witnessing an argument between a man and woman on the street escalate into physical violence, from my mother's warning. I cannot recall my mother describing any other behavior—and that included womanizing, boozing, and chronic unemployment—as so heinous that it was irreparable, could not be corrected or even smoothed over by any amount of talking, crying, or patience, where a woman's only recourse was to get away from the man as rapidly as possible. When I was growing up, there was no such term as domestic violence. Men hitting women in the privacy of their homes wasn't something that was publicly discussed. But I grew up with three siblings, two of them brothers, and had or witnessed enough fights to know battling wasn't my strong suit, that physical violence was to be avoided, as much because I wasn't good at it as because fighting was, as my parents always said, both wrong and no way to solve anything. Early on, I cobbled together an assault-free woman type from whole cloth. I was tall and not small, so it seemed to me that physical size worked for me. I'd seen enough fights between boys growing up to know that men didn't necessarily follow the rule and pick on someone their own size, but usually someone smaller. Because of this, I have tended to choose men who, just to be safe, are about my physical size, subconsciously looking for an even match, consciously for none at all. I honed my verbal skills as a way to attack and defend myself nonviolently, became proficient at selling woof tickets, casting the verbal barb, a master of the fine art of the dis. As added protection, I also strove to be financially independent, so at best I'd never tolerate abuse from a man because I was economically dependent upon him, and at least I'd have carfare to leave if he failed to realize I wasn't the type of woman who got hit and dared to raise his hand to me. And you know, as absurd as I now know this or any other strategy is, I actually thought it was working. For years, no man ever laid a hand on me. I thought I was home free. In 1983 I even married my future assailant, a man who was bigger than I was, a teacher, and went to live with him at an all-girls school where he taught. Even as a wife, I had no intention of being domesticated or being a victim of domestic violence, I was a career girl, already had a child, was reasonably successful. In hindsight, I recognize I got married just to try it, so I could cross off another of the talismans of womanhood with a smug "Been there, done that." I wasn't thinking about either "Till death do us part" or the price marriage might require I pay. And for a year I didn't think about violence, was convinced I'd successfully navigated past the whole business. Until one day my husband said, "Jill. I want to adopt Carol." (Not her real name.) And I said, "Carol who?" Making sure, because once at the dinner table my husband asked excitedly, "Did you hear what happened to Erica?" and when I said, "Erica who?" he snapped, "Erica from 'All My Children'!" I have learned that it is important to be clear if he's talking about real people or characters on television.

"Carol who's in my class," he barks. Right, I remember, young woman from a foster home, very bright, friendly, plain-looking, needy.

"You've got to be kidding," I say, and chuckle, but when he twirls around and I see his face, think to myself, "Uh, oh. This is no joke."

"Why not?" he snaps. "She has no family, she really likes both of us and the kids, and it would provide her with a family." It is, I think, hard enough to blend the two of us, his daughter by a previous marriage, and mine, into a family, but I don't say that. Instead, I say,

"A family? Isn't she about to go to college?" As I remember, college was the great escape from the constraints of family, but that was ten years ago, maybe I'm out of touch.

"Yes, but what does that have to do with it? She'll need someone to call from school, someplace to come on vacations, people to counsel her."

"I don't think it's a very good idea. We've got two adolescent daughters we can barely counsel now," I say.

"Fuck that, they're spoiled, have had all the privileges, they'll be fine. I'm talking about taking in a young girl who's had nothing but a hard time." My husband dismisses my protest with a sentence on our decidedly tenuous economic status. You'd think as an educator he'd have figured out there are no guarantees. Christ, you'd think he'd have figured that out living with me.

"Doesn't she have a college scholarship?" I ask. I'm not denying the girl's had a hard time, but she's smart, ambitious, cunning, doesn't need us.

"So fucking what? What she needs is a family. I know how important that is. Remember, I was adopted." There's that old trump card, the A-word, my cue to shut up and mind my own fucking grew-up-with-my-birth-parents business. It's like when childless people say something critical about children and some nursing mother snaps, "Well, you're not a mother." Yeah, yeah, you were adopted, but you were three, not seventeen, and your parents got you from an orphanage, not out of the classroom of an elite prep school. But of course I don't say that. Instead I say, "But she's seventeen. Isn't that a little old for adoption?"

I guess I might as well have said what I was thinking, because my husband picks up the sarcasm behind my words, snarls, "What the hell difference does it make how old she is? She still needs a loving family," adds nastily, "You of all people should know that," which I rightly take to be a crack on me and mine. And them, asshole, is fightin' words.

"Yeah, yeah. But don't you think it's a little strange for a forty-year-old man to adopt a seventeen-year-old high-school girl?"

"No, I don't," he yells. "Strange to who? Who cares what any-one thinks?"

"Well, I hope you care what I think, because I'm your wife and I think it's strange. I don't want to do it."

He looks at me with contempt. "That is so goddamn selfish. You have been raised with all the privileges. Miss Bourgeoisie, Miss Martha's Vineyard, and you're too fucking selfish and insecure to share it with someone else. That's the trouble with the fucking black middle class . . ." I look at him incredulously. Hey, I'm no stranger to the black bourgeoisie and its problems, nor am I in denial, but somehow I don't think refusal to adopt nearly adult nymphets is high on the list of the psychopathologies of bourgie Negroes. Plus, I'm thirty-two years old, and have just about had it with being whipped by black folks for being middle class, particularly when the one doing the whipping is my very middle-class husband. The only difference between us is that he worked his way into the bour-geoisie, I was born there. But I'm trying to keep my marriage to-gether, although it has only been thirteen months and things are not looking good, so I don't say that. Instead, I say,

"I don't think it's selfish. We've got our hands full with our two daughters when she's with us, not to mention trying to make our marriage work . . ." My voice drifts off, no doubt searching for words. In vain. There's nothing there but white noise.

"Jill, I am really serious about this adoption," he says, walking toward me. "And if you can't support me in this, I have real ques-tions about whether or not our marriage can work." Maybe it's my ears, but that sounds like a threat to me. After all the laughs, strug-gles over money, holidays spent together, housekeeping, deep soul-to-soul conversations, sex, the blending of old friends and making of new ones, this, as they say in Hollywood, is the deal breaker: adopt Carol or divorce. My husband stares into my eyes, glaring. His face is slightly red, his lips full and dark, the way they get when we're making love. "Well? Well? What's it gonna be?" he yells.

And even though I don't have any incidence of it, then or now, it's the only way I could fathom his existence: so I say, "Wait a minute. Are you fucking her?" And that's when he slaps me upside my head with his open palm so hard I see red, white, and blue stars and my ear rings for twenty-four hours.

In the end, my husband doesn't answer the question, we don't adopt Carol, I take my mother's advice and leave not long after that. I occasionally see my ex-husband's raging face when I'm swimming and my right ear starts bothering me, a result of a punctured eardrum, his legacy to me.

But more than the eardrum—which healed—and my mother's adages—which linger—the lesson most profoundly learned in that moment was that there is no type of woman who is assaulted by men. If a man's going to hit, there are too many fish in the sea to bother with finding a type. There is no type, because we're all the type. Being on the receiving end of violence has made me permanently more sensitive to everyday violence, not just the big, dramatic, undeniable violence of war, famine, genocide, getting hit by hubby dearest, but the everyday violence that this culture inflicts upon women. It is this casual, nuanced, insidious violence that impacts upon all women, whatever our politics or race or type. It's just that until I got walloped, more often than not I didn't recognize it for what it is.

As a woman, and particularly as an African American woman, violence is very much on my mind. How can it not be now that I understand that the personal, subjective, so-called "domestic" violence is inextricably bound to the seemingly impersonal, objective, public political violence that runs rampant in American culture. There is no way to separate the personal from the political, since one feeds off and informs the other, they are in a symbiotic relationship. Violence is with me every morning when I pick up the newspaper and read about the latest attack by the local or federal government on entitlement programs benefiting women and children. Or when I read about efforts to curtail a woman's right to abortion or force women receiving welfare benefits to put their children in day care and work for the city in some latter-day incarnation of slavery. It is with me when I turn on the television and watch the news, filled with images of demonized black women, images created to justify the latest cuts and abdication of government responsibility. Read reports of yet another woman raped, beaten, or killed, another woman working and living in poverty. When I watch music videos, which isn't often, I am inundated with images of black women dismembered by twisted, violent, male sexual fantasies. In music videos there is seldom any whole black woman, merely parts. We are portrayed as "Butt," or "Tits," or spread-legged "Pussy," barely dressed, contorted sperm receptacles, an array of disconnected body parts to be used and abused at the whim of men. When I turn the channel again, in search of an entertainment program, it is nearly impossible to be entertained. The representations of black women on commercial television are limited to objects of ridicule, victims, and mulatto sex objects, though occasionally we are portrayed as ballbusting, emasculating authority figures.

The radio offers no relief, no better. The right-wing ideologues use us as archetypes to illustrate and explain the collapse of the American family, culture, society, and economy. The rappers portray us as "Bitches," "Hos" and "Skeazers." The crooners, professing affection and benevolence, configure us as passive love objects and sperm receptacles. So, I turn off all the media and decide to go outside. But first, I have to get dressed, and once again, I am surrounded by violence. Because I am an African American woman in a culture that devalues all women, and values women of color least of all, when I get dressed, my choices are not, as they should be, simply ones of comfort and adornment. By necessity, I must also dress to protect, defend myself from the male violence that is always around me. On the street, in public, that violence can take many forms, from catcalls and obscene remarks by male passersby to beating, rape, and murder. Knowing this, I dress accordingly, protectively. Shoes I can run in if I have to. Skirts not too short. A shawl or scarf whose original function is to provide warmth but that I instead use protectively, to cover a glimpse of cleavage, bare arm, whatever might provoke men's violence, even knowing that it needs no provocation from me, that the rape is about violence, not sex. Perhaps pathetically, I do this to feel proactive, refuse to succumb to the powerlessness of always reacting, bolster myself with the delusion that if I make myself less noticeable the odds will tilt slightly in my favor. Thus armored, I go out into the world. But no matter what I do, the violence is unavoidable. It comes from places both expected and unimagined.

As a black woman, the violence I feel often comes from the assault of erasure and invisibility, of being the last person waited upon, or the one for whom the door is not held, or the woman whose opinion is never solicited because others literally do not see me. It comes casually, when a cashier in a store ignores me in the front of the line to serve other customers and when I say something, jumps, starts, looks at all five feet eight of me and says, "Oh, I didn't see you." Or walking the street and having no one step aside for me, make eye contact, stop their car while turning and let me cross the street.

Sometimes, there is the violence summoned by being visible to men as an objectified, sexualized thing. Lost in happy thought, a perfectly wonderful day is verbally assaulted because I did not hear a man speak to me, did not speak to him, or maybe I did hear him call, "Hey, mama with the big legs!" but chose not to respond. His violence toward me then is verbal, something along the lines of "Well, fuck you, bitch. Your legs aren't shit, anyway." What I'd like to say is, "No one asked you, dickhead," but I don't, feel in a desperate way as if I got over, escaped, because his violence was limited to words. I am torn between the desire to be seen, heard, and appreciated, and the tendency to cower within my black female invisibility, knowing that even though to be invisible is a constant source of pain and rage, to be noticed only as a representation of something men can use at will is far more dangerous.

Still, when I get home in one physical piece, however affronted, I know that I am one of the lucky ones. For too many women, every day the violence takes the form of a purse snatched, face beaten, body raped, a woman murdered. I know only a handful of women, of any color, who have not been hit by a man. I do not know any who have not been verbally abused, either by a loved one or an anonymous man on the street. I know more than a few women who have been raped, most often in their own homes, by some man they thought they knew or wanted to know.

Often, I return home from these forays outside tired, defeated, depressed. I close the door to my apartment and breathe a sigh of relief. But then the doorbell or telephone rings. And it's a black man calling to talk about the problems in his life, not bothering to ask even, "How are you?" When I do get a word in edgewise, tell him a little about my day, as often as not it's as if he literally doesn't hear me, keeps on talking about himself, or says something like, "Look. Everyone knows black women have it easy. Have the jobs. That you all are getting over at our expense." And in that moment lies the confluence of the personal and the political: The negative media and political representations of black women as emasculating matriarchs responsible for the problems of black men invade my house in the form of a man dismissing my reality as less important than his. Really, isn't denial of black women's lives and experience just another insidious form of violence? So the cycle of violence starts again. Too often, sleep is not even an escape because my psyche is so filled with an hour's, a day's, a lifetime's worth of violent images and acts that I have nightmares, violent dreams.

For the most part, the violence in my life is the violence of negation, misrepresentation, and invisibility, although the possibility of physical violence is ever present. But the emotional, spiritual, economic, political, intellectual violence is violence nonetheless, and also deadly. It slowly kills the spirit, twists the soul, makes dreams impossible. More often than not, it is the thoughtless, offhand violence of casual disrespect: a request ignored, opinion dismissed, comment not responded to. On a day-to-day basis, it is this offhand violence that is most devastating. The big events and major eruptions I can separate from the daily fabric of my life, declare tragic exceptions to some vague notion of how I see myself, label crisis. It is the casual, everyday violence that needs no provocation and from which I must constantly protect myself that truly erodes my soul. It determines where I go and when, what I wear, my responses to the people around me, relentlessly wears away my sense of self and safety in the world.

Violence against women in this culture is systemic, it affects every facet of our lives, even when we are unaware of it. Sometimes, when it is physical, it rapidly and literally kills us. The political violence of the right wing every day moves closer to starving and marginalizing us—and our children—slowly. The brutalized, sexualized, victimized, and occasionally victimizing images of women in the mass media kill our realities, our dignity, our very selves. Representations of black women and other women of color as lazy, destructive, basically problematic forces in the culture foster and encourage a climate in which we are without value. What does it matter if you abuse, beat, even kill women who are usually invisible and when we're seen are nothing but trouble? All these elements work together to create a climate in which violence toward black women, both literal and figurative, is not only acceptable and understandable, but somehow okay.

In the past several decades, largely as a result of the work of feminists, the issue of violence against women—I try not to use the term "domestic violence," since I think it conjures up some place-specific, private, little hush-hush problem, when the real issue is everywhere, large, and needs to become very public—has become an important conversation in the white community. Unfortunately, the same is not true in the black community. As a group, black men and, heartbreakingly, many black women, refuse to acknowledge and confront violence toward women or, truth be told, any other issue that specifically affects black women. To be concerned with any gender issue is, by and large, still dismissed as a "white woman's thing," as if black men in America, or anywhere else in the world, for that matter, have managed to avoid the contempt for women that is a fundamental element of living in a patriarchy. Even when lip service is given to sexism as a valid concern, it is at best a secondary issue. First and foremost is racism and the ways in which it impacts black men. It is the naive belief of many that once racism is eradicated, sexism, and its unnatural outgrowth, violence toward women, will miraculously melt away, as if the abuse of women is solely an outgrowth of racism and racial oppression. As much as black folks love to call upon glowing, idealized images of the African Motherland when those pictures are comforting, no one wants to talk about the persistence of violence toward women in South Africa post-apartheid. Anyway, there's no need to go that far, there's plenty of violence in our own backyards, communities, bedrooms.

As a group, black Americans dismiss violence toward women, sexism, and any other issues that impact solely or primarily on women as unimportant, a mere casual afterthought to the real important business of racism and how it affects black men. Yet another one of our race secrets. But for me there is no way to separate racism from sexism. Don't ask me when I wake up in the morning and see my reflection in the bathroom mirror, which do I see first, a black person or a woman? It's like that old question about which came first, the chicken or the egg? Who knows? Who cares? What is the point of this conversation? The truth of the matter is that when it comes to black men, even factoring in prejudices based on color, class, looks, and personality, I know that overwhelmingly when the brothers discriminate against, dis, harass, take advantage of, or verbally or physically abuse me, they do so based on my gender. And that's sexism. What makes black men think they can be born and raised in a culture that has profound contempt for all women and places black women at the bottom, and escape unaffected? You never hear a black man say it is possible to be unaffected by racism, do you?

In fact, it is precisely the effect of racism on black men that encourages the denial of gender issues and the oppression of women. Just as one of the pillars of slavery and plantation life was the emasculation of black men as husbands, fathers, or males capable of the basic functions of providing for and protecting themselves or anyone else, one of the functions of the post-slavery black community, and black women in particular, has been the restoration of manhood. Our job became to make black men feel like men by making sure we didn't dominate, intimidate, or, like ol' Massa, emasculate. Under the dangerous and mistaken assumption that manhood is defined by a man's ability to control and oppress women, too often black men seek to fit themselves into tired white patriarchal modes of behavior. It doesn't work, and black men become increasingly frustrated with, alienated from, and sometimes violent toward black women.

Most often it is wives, girlfriends, and partners who are the recipients of black men's rage. We are women, easy targets, and if we are women of color and poor, the likelihood of our victimization increases dramatically. According to a report released in March 1997 conducted by the New York City Department of Health, 49 percent of women murdered were killed by husbands or boyfriends, usually incredibly savagely, half of them in their own homes. This number is larger than those for women slain in robberies, drug-related violence, sexual assaults, disputes, random attacks, or any other circumstance. Of women murdered over the five-year period studied, 52 percent were black and 29 percent Latina, even though combined we are only half of the city's female population. White women, who comprise half the population of women in New York City, account for just 16 percent of those murdered. Nationally, 40 percent of murdered women are killed by intimates.

If the culture does not even pretend to value black women's lives, why should our men? For that matter, why should we value ourselves? The truth is that it is often impossible for black men to acknowledge and understand the relationship between sexism and violence. It's a lot easier to solely blame racism for all our problems, internal and external, than to confront the ways in which men perpetuate and collude in the oppression of black women. The ways, in the name of patriarchy and sexism, that black men diminish, oppress, and sometimes kill black women. We need to face reality and get down to the business of setting our African American house in order. Only then will we have any success on other battlefields.

First there has to be acknowledgment, particularly by men, but by women as well, that sexism exists, and that it is just as unhealthy and destructive to self and community as racism. In a wonderful letter I received in the summer of 1995 from the Reverend Eugene Rivers, a young, progressive minister in Boston, he wrote, "As a people, we appear confused and lost when it comes to fighting the duality of racism and sexism. It seems that black women are always sacrificed on the altar of racial solidarity. We have some mistaken notion that standing up against sexism in all its forms constitutes being disloyal to black men. Fighting sexism goes hand in hand with fighting an oppressive system that has damaged all African Americans who share the unique American legacy of slavery. The sanctity of black women has been historically violated by too many slave owners, overseers, and sons of plantation owners who have either forced themselves on black female slaves or beaten them to make them 'obey.' Why would black men want to emulate any form of behavior responsible for enslaving them hundreds of years ago and still enslaves them today?"

But if the overwhelming majority of representations of black women in the social and political culture are negative, why should black men or anyone else value us, respect us, or place us at the center of anything? When was the last time you can recall a black woman being accorded either the attention or sympathetic status of white woman victims of male violence like Nicole Brown Simpson, the jogger brutally beaten in Central Park in 1989, or even Sunny von Bulow, the comatose heiress whose husband was tried and acquitted for her attempted murder? Black women are seldom figures who elicit either sympathy or support, much less become cause célèbres, whatever their status. From fired Surgeon General Joycelyn Elders to withdrawn Justice Department nominee Lani Guinier to victim of sexual harassment Anita Hill, down to Eleanor Bumpers, a sixty-seven-year-old grandmother shot a dozen times by New York City police in 1986 (one officer was tried and subsequently acquitted), black women are not viewed as important, nor is the violence done against us. If the dominant culture communicates, either directly or through its actions, that the lives of black women are unimportant, that it does not intend to protect us, why would anyone—including black men, or, for that matter, black women—feel otherwise?

In Narcotics Anonymous they say that everyone has their bottom, the point at which they decide enough is too much, stop messing with drugs, and start working those twelve steps. But the descent to the bottom isn't like taking the down escalator in Macy's; you don't usually know you're descending and can't see the trappings of your demise as you make your way down. I wasn't aware of the ways in which everyday violence surrounds, touches, and wears me down until I got popped in the head. My husband's fist opened up an enormous section of my mind I didn't even know existed, the place where I stuffed away the everyday violence experienced in my life and observed in the lives of women around me, then sealed with a strip of tape stamped with the words "I'm Not the Type." This awareness of everyday violence is painful, not easy to live with. It is as if a protective layer of skin has been peeled away and I have become hypersensitive. In defense, I have drawn new lines around every area of my life and do not let people, particularly men, inside as easily as I once did. I watch the men I know or meet for signs of verbal, emotional, or physical violence toward women. When I see it I call them on it or cut them loose. I spend more and more time in the company of those, mostly women, as sensitive to everyday violence as I am.

So of course it was one of my girls who called me up one morning in late May of 1995 and said, "You're not going to believe this. Have you heard Reverend Al Sharpton, Don King, Congressman Charlie Rangel, and the boys want to give Mike Tyson a parade and hero's welcome in Harlem?" "Over my dead body," I said, "not while I'm living here."

A few days later I read a story in the *New York Amsterdam News,* a newspaper owned by opportunist-in-soul-brother's-clothing Bill Tatum, which touts itself, without progressive politics, explanation, or punctuation, as "ThenewBlackview," detailing the planned event under the headline "Stars, a parade, a street festival for the champ," and listing members of the welcoming committee. What was the occasion for celebration? Ex-heavyweight champion Mike Tyson had just been released from prison after being convicted of rape and serving three years and he needed to promote his upcoming fight, the most expensive event ever on pay per view. What better way than to parade him through Harlem, the capital of black America? Who was hosting the party? Many were ministers, among them Wyatt Tee Walker of Harlem's Canaan Baptist Church, and Conrad Muhammed from the Nation of Islam, neither of which are organizations known for fighting for the rights of women. A few were unelected leaders, like minister-without-a-church and former-FBI-wire-wearer Reverend Al Sharpton. The only woman on the committee was the singer Roberta Flack, don't ask me why.

I could say my initial response when I learned of the planned TysonFest was surprise, but I'd be lying. It has been a long time since I've been shocked by anyone's—and, sad to say, that includes black men's—denial, disrespect, and sometimes total contempt for black women. These days what surprises me is a brother who's sensitive to women's issues.

Within a few days of hearing of the planned TysonFest, a coalition of women and men, African Americans Against Violence (AAAV), formed. The original objective was to stop the parade, rally, street festival, and conferring of hero status on longtime black woman abuser and convicted rapist Mike Tyson, using Harlem as a historically resonate backdrop and its people as unpaid extras. We were an eclectic group, some familiar faces, others not. Most of those present were activists; some ran activist organizations. Nearly everyone had a history of involvement in social justice issues. The median age was probably forty, although our oldest member was over seventy, our youngest seventeen. The only elected officials who supported us early on and actively were Harlem City Councilwoman C. Virginia Fields, a black woman, and Assembly member Keith L. T. Wright. The only member of the local religious community who supported our efforts was the Reverend Calvin O. Butts, pastor of Harlem's Abyssinian Baptist Church. The rest of them didn't even return our phone calls, a slap in the face to black women, who are the black church. It was immediately clear that we had to organize around the older, larger, more important issue, for which Mike Tyson was simply the latest poster boy: the refusal of black men in particular and black people in general to recognize and take responsibility for violence against black women and girls. The screaming subtext was that black women don't matter to black men except as supporters, coddlers, welcoming vaginas, colluders-in-their-own-oppression, and occasionally, usually at public events, convenient icons.

The issue was never Tyson's right to fight or his entitlement to a second chance. If Tyson chooses to make his living as a boxer, likes to, as he's said, push people's noses into their brain pans, that's his disturbing personal choice. The issue was the message presenting a spectacle in his honor sends to women, children, and men. Since when did being convicted of a crime and serving time warrant a hero's welcome? In terms of the planned public hoopla, how could our male elected officials, clergy, and community leaders participate in such a cynical spectacle, particularly since all of these men are where they are as a result of the work, votes, and on the backs of black women. What could those preachers be thinking every Sunday when they looked out on their overwhelmingly female congregants? Are they so complacent and corrupt that they too don't see black women even when we're the ones signing the checks?

In the African American community, a pervasive legacy of the last two decades of unremitting attack on black people, poor people, people of color, women, gays, progressives, and democracy personified by Reagan and Bush, and the steady elimination of any safety net of social programs, has been the creation of a profound dichotomy between the people and those whose job it is to lead them. The people have become despairing, hopeless, and enraged. Our leaders have become cynical, opportunistic, and corrupt. As *New York Times* columnist Robert Lipsyte wrote on June 18, 1995, "The welcome-back party for Mike Tyson seems to have fizzled from a Harlem parade and street festival next Tuesday to what it always really was, a photo op/press conference outside the Apollo Theater for Don King and Showtime to boost their rapist in the rankings." The cynical subtext was the sanitizing of Tyson in order to obtain commercial endorsements, where the real, long money is for athletes, à la Michael Jordan. Can you imagine the specter of Mike Tyson selling Snapple, McDonald's, maybe doing a Public Service Announcement for safe sex? Initially, there was talk of Tyson giving away a million dollars to youth programs in New York. The truth was he pledged to give a million dollars to youth programs nationally, presumably after he and promoter, convicted felon, and man of the electrified hair Don King, who served time for stomping an African American man to death, took their Mike-Tyson's-a-Hero dog and pony show to your hometown. A million dollars total. Not much when you think that Tyson stood to make at least $25 million from the title bout. It was the underlying and more enduring message of such actions that was far more disturbing: that violence against black women does not much matter, and to the extent it does it can be erased by a few dollars strategically dropped.

One wonders what Desiree Washington, eighteen at the time of her rape by Tyson, thought of all this. Washington was demonized when her allegations were made public. Her attackers went into that old, tired, blame-the-victim mode. Depending on who in the black community you talked to and their gender, Desiree Washington "asked for it," because she "shouldn't have been in his room," since "you know what a man wants that time of night." This all added up to the conclusion that as a result of being in the wrong place at the wrong time she "got what she deserved." All else failing, there was the old standby, made infamous regarding Rasheeda Moore, the crack-wielding temptress who lured Boy Scout D.C. Mayor Marion Barry to his day of reckoning with the Feds at the Vista Hotel, and emblazoned on T-shirts wildly popular in Chocolate City, "The bitch set me up."

Both men and women proclaimed loud and clear what many women already feared: that in the eyes of many, black women have no rights that a man need respect. The legal fact, generally accepted in the white community vis à vis white women, albeit with great resistance and grumbling, that whenever a woman says No! she means No!, simply didn't apply to black women. Using this rationale, neither Desiree Washington nor any of the rest of us have the right to make a bad decision and change our minds, at least not when a penis is involved. Congratulations! You have just been selected Miss Black America! Please leave your vocal cords, brain, and self-respect at the door. Once inside you can pick up your new wardrobe: silence, obedience, and the shroud of our male fantasies, sexual, violent, and otherwise! My nominee for most offensive remark is that of a black man who asked me, "If it was rape, why didn't she fight him off?" I suggested to him that if he didn't want to have sex and Mike Tyson did, I was confident he'd turn over, spread 'em, and apply the KY jelly himself.

For those who insist on crying racism—the great absolver of black male responsibility—citing Indiana as the birthplace of the Ku Klux Klan, moaning about Mike's inadequate legal representation—and let me say this: he paid enough for it, is it my fault that he was too stupid to hire winning counsel?—and making other excuses for Tyson's conviction on charges of raping Desiree Washington, I say: Mike Tyson has a history of violent and abusive behavior toward black women. If you don't believe me, dig this quote from boxer Jose Torres' biography of Mike, in which he quotes him as describing a punch he delivered to then-wife Robin Givens, "She flew backward, hitting every fucking wall in the apartment." If this doesn't move you because you subscribe to the Robin Givens is a bitch-goddess-gold-digging-ho-who-deserves-whatever-she-got theory, Torres also quotes Tyson as saying, "You know something, I like to hurt women when I make love to them . . . I like to hear them scream with pain, to see them bleed . . . It gives me pleasure."

I wasn't surprised when I heard the boys wanted to make Mike a hero, hold him up as a role model to our children. I was first sad, then sick, then angry. Born, raised, and living in Harlem, if I didn't take a stand I'd have to pack my bags and move. To stay silent was to collude in my own victimization. As Bob Herbert wrote in his column in the *New York Times,* "For black women in particular, any kind of celebration of Mike Tyson is an act of contempt. It gives comfort and support to the idea—expressed so frequently in the rap culture and acted out so tragically often in the real world—that women are here primarily for two reasons: to serve men as vessels of pleasure and as objects to be brutalized." (June 10, 1995.)

It is always difficult to say why a particular event or moment or circumstance galvanizes ordinary people to take action. The planned celebration of Mike Tyson was a moment in which many of the strands that make up the fabric of everyday violence against black women came together. Verbal abuse, emotional and psychological harassment, threats of physical violence, negation of gender issues, and, of course, the physical assault of rape. For those already sensitive to everyday violence, the event was a total overload. The issue wasn't was it possible to do something, but that it was impossible not to. Once committed to action, organizing basically requires three things: a goal, a strategy, and people willing to do the work. At the first meeting, we drafted a statement articulating why we found the planned event "inappropriate, offensive, and unacceptable," for distribution to the media and community. It was rapidly decided that we would hold a vigil for women who had been victims of violence and abuse on June 19, the day before the planned Tyson event.

Al Sharpton, who was heading up the Tyson celebration, launched a full-scale personal attack on those of us who dared to suggest that Mike was not hero material and that black women's rights must be respected. We were called elitists, dupes of the white media, outsiders, and political opportunists. People received threatening calls at home and at work. There was the familiar, tired accusation that we were race traitors, trying to tear "The Black Man" down. Jesus, you'd think "The Black Man" was some towering monolith, cast in stone and immovable, perfect, unflawed, frozen in a pose of unassailable righteousness. Why is it that when black women stand up for ourselves we're accused of attacking black men? Is it that we have no role other than as adjuncts, supporters, appendages? Well, here's what I say to those backward brothers: If your penis needs maintenance, go to a urologist, that's not my job.

Some of the contempt and suspicion with which most men responded to those opposed to the Tyson celebration can also be traced to black women's voicelessness, our silence in the face of the everyday violence that surrounds us. Given that too much of the time we do not fight violence but instead tolerate it, I can understand men's surprise and resentment of the collective cry of protest in the summer of 1995. Why did it happen then, when violence against women is such an everyday thing? At that moment a group of us reached a collective bottom, had simply had enough, were mad as hell, and wouldn't take any more.

June 19, the day of the vigil, was one of the hottest yet, high nineties. It got hotter than that in my air-conditioned apartment when I called a former lover who I mistakenly thought was a current friend, I guess in the twisted hope that he'd be supportive, reassuring, address that great need of women and "be there for me," and he said, "I think what you're doing is wrong. You should leave Mike Tyson alone. He's served his time, doesn't he have a right to fight?"

"Sure. We never said he didn't. Our point is that he shouldn't be proclaimed a hero by our so-called leaders and elected officials. In all our statements we've said we support his right to transformation and redemption—" He interrupts.

"Huh! That's what you say, but do you really believe that? Come on."

"Yeah. I do."

"Then why are you having this anti-Tyson march?"

"It's not anti-Tyson, it's pro–black women. There's a difference."

"So you say," he sneers. "I know you."

"Well, I gotta go to the vigil . . ." Perhaps this is the moment I remember once and for all that lovers who are not available in times of need become exes.

"Wait! I wasn't going to tell you this, but I think you're in danger," he says.

"From whom?"

"I'm not going to name names, but I've gotten maybe thirty calls in the last few days from people who know I know you saying, 'What's your girl doing? She's fucking with the brother. She'd better be careful or she'll get hurt. Tell her to stop fuckin' with Mike.' "

I laugh, uncomfortably. "Let me assure you I have no interest in fucking with Mike, on any level. Are you suggesting I'm going to be assassinated for standing up for my rights as a black woman?"

"I don't know. There could be trouble, there're a lot of crazy people out on the streets."

"So I should not go, cower in my apartment, what?" I yell.

"Cancel, reschedule, do it next week, not tonight, the day before Mike's homecoming," he says.

"I can't do that. Are you coming to the vigil to protect me?" I ask. Abruptly, cat's got Mr. Talkative's tongue.

I hang up, but I'm shaken. I tell a few members of the committee about the alleged threats and we beef up security. When I tell Bill Lynch, longtime political operative, union organizer, architect of David Dinkins' successful 1989 New York mayoral campaign, friend, and budding feminist about the conversation, he makes a sound between a laugh and a snort. "C'mon, Nelse, don't get pulled into that. They've tried everything else, and now it's the threat of physical violence? If you cave now, they've won."

"You're right," I say.

"Besides, whoever told you that was no friend of yours. If he was, he would've said he'd be out there tonight with five guys."

"So, you don't think I'll be shot in the head tonight?"

"Naaawww," Bill drawls, then snickers, "But if you are, Al better forget it. He'll be answering for this for the rest of his life." I go, I live.

The evening after the vigil I arrive home exhausted and ener-gized, a battle won, the war still raging. The organizing around Tyson was another step in black women seizing voice, setting con-text, taking leadership, framing the issue. For two weeks we suc-ceeded in creating a dialogue around the issue of violence against black women, with black women visible and in leadership. We built an effective coalition of African Americans from diverse political, re-ligious, class, sexual, and cultural perspectives. But it was only a small step, a brief, specific action; the long-term hard work of or-ganizing, acting, and educating against violence continues.

Once woken up to see the everyday nature of violence, it is im-possible to ignore, in all its guises. It does not matter if it is the physical violence of being smacked in the head, or a bunch of men deciding to declare a convicted rapist a hero, or the casual, verbal vi-olence of being sexualized, objectified, and humiliated by unknown men on the street. It is also impossible to fight every battle. I try and choose mine wisely, according to where I can be most effective, make the greatest impact, move forward. I will not accept secondary status when it comes to men, but I am not always or only their ad-versary. I struggle to keep the part of me that is soft and loving in-tact and available even as I recognize and fight against the violence all around me, to not flinch defensively when a man grabs my arm and turns me around to tell me he loves me. My feminism is not di-dactic, but pragmatic. I have learned not to sweat many of the small things. I am, I hope, aware but not reactionary.

Ever since I was a little girl, my mother has told me I feel too much, have too much of what Mom, the high-school and college student of German, called weltschmerz, the depression or apathy that comes from the contradiction between the way the world is and the way it could be.

My mother's solution was to suggest I learn to put some of

what bothers me "in the back of your mind, where the tissue paper is." But I never had much mental tissue paper. Now I have none, the last of it dislodged years ago by my husband's fist.

Two months after the vigil, on Saturday, August 19, 1995, the same day Mike Tyson made—earned just isn't the right word—$25 million in less than a minute and a half in a mock fight against a chump named Peter McNeeley, a thirty-three-year-old black woman named Deletha Word leapt from Detroit's Belle Isle Bridge and died in what must have been absolute terror. Deletha Word could not swim.

In the early morning hours of August 19, Word drove on after a minor accident with a car driven by nineteen-year-old Martell Welch. Welch, with two friends in tow, pursued. Word, apparently panicked, stopped, backed into Welch's car, then stopped again. According to news reports, Welch pulled her from the car, ripped off some of her clothes, and commenced beating her. Then he got a jack from the trunk of his car and began beating Word's car. Terrified, Word ran away and climbed onto the railing of the bridge. Welch's friends chanted, "Jump, bitch, jump!" At least twenty-six bystanders did nothing to help Deletha Word. She jumped. Two black men came upon the scene, dove into the water, and tried to save her. Her body was later found ten miles away, one of her legs amputated, apparently by a boat propeller. The Detroit police allowed Welch and his friends to drive away. He was not arrested until thirty hours later. Deletha Word left behind a thirteen-year-old daughter.

I cry like a baby when I hear about Deletha Word. Then I tremble with a rage so fierce my whole body vibrates. Then I go and swim for an hour and fifteen minutes. Afterward, even though I am eager to get home and lock the door, I do not drive fast and aggressively as I usually do, but slowly, cautiously, suddenly aware of another aspect of everyday violence, that for a black woman, a fender bender can mean death.

Months later, I still dream of Deletha Word, balanced on that railing, filled with terror, fall with her through dark, cold air toward water, and like a child, awaken before impact. Is it true what my mother told me as a little girl, that you never see yourself die in dreams because the shock would kill you? What I do know is that wide awake, minding my business, everyday violence can sneak up on me unawares, just as it did Deletha Word, and like her I cannot wake up and escape, have no doubt that it can kill me. Perhaps I am powerless against the violent nightmares that come to me when I am sleeping, reminders, I think, of the real, everyday violence that awaits me when I arise, reminders of the need to fight against it, to wake up and live.

THE MARCH, THE MATRIARCHS, AND
GROWN-UP BLACK WOMEN

IT IS HARD TO REMEMBER A TIME when I was without Aretha Franklin, she is to my life what Dinah Washington was for my mother, Duke Ellington for my father, the ever present musical punctuation and subtext, my personal amen chorus. Depending on what is going on in my world, more often than not I listen to Aretha's songs selectively. Years have gone by in which I skip over the slow, sad, love dirges, unable to hear "I Never Loved a Man (The Way I Love You)," or "Do Right Woman, Do Right Man," without feeling victimized and wincing.

The Queen of Soul is never absent, simply edited. The upbeat and danceable "Since You've Been Gone," "Eleanor Rigby," and "Spanish Harlem" blare through my rooms, I sing along and dance alone. Aretha's always strong and beautiful pipes keep me sane. Aretha's voice is the constant, yet there is only one song of hers that transcends every mood, "Respect."

What you want, baby I've got it/
What you need, you know I've got it/
All I'm asking for is a little respect/baby,
When you come home.

"Respect" is not only my personal mantra, it is the unofficial, collective anthem of an invisible nation of silent black women, yearning as we have been to make our feelings heard and understood as Aretha does, for the respect of others. I am sure it is time we stopped asking for and demanded and seized these things, but this is only possible if we speak up. Otherwise, we relegate ourselves to receiving only what men want us to have. Ancient and recent history should have taught us that this is not a good thing.

Where were even a few of the righteous black men who swarmed to Washington for the Million Man March, bent on a testosterone-inspired orgy of male bonding and atonement, when Rosa Parks, mother of the civil rights movement, was beaten and her home burglarized in Detroit in 1994? If just a few thousand of the million men had been in Harlem's Audubon Ballroom on February 21, 1965, it's likely those assassins wouldn't have been able to get such a clear shot at Malcolm X, and Betty Shabazz wouldn't have been left broke, alone, and with six daughters to raise. Was her presence at Louis Farrakhan's finest hour the price Shabazz was required to pay to keep her daughter out of jail? On January 13, 1995, Quibilah Shabazz was arrested in Minneapolis and charged with conspiring to hire a hit man to assassinate Louis Farrakhan, whom she, and at least one time, her mother, believed was involved in her father's assassination. (Despite the inflammatory statements about Malcolm X he has made, Farrakhan has denied any such involvement.) The so-called "hit man" Quibilah hired, Michael Fitzpatrick, was, in fact, a longtime government informant who subsequently disappeared into the federal Witness Protection Program. Charges were eventually dropped after Farrakhan and others suggested that the whole scheme was a frame-up by the FBI and other police authorities. The government agreed to drop the charges against her if Shabazz, the single parent of a son named Malcolm, living on welfare, went into drug treatment and committed no crimes for a period of two years. (On June 1, 1997, Betty Shabazz sustained burns over 80 percent of her body in a fire in her Yonkers, New York, apartment allegedly set by her grandson, Malcolm. In addition to being a tragedy for Shabazz, the fire emphasizes the physical, emotional, and psychological vulnerability of generations of descendents of American martyrs.)

And Queen Mother Moore, aging icon of the long defunct black nationalist movement, hauled out through the 1960s and 70s when men needed a woman to integrate the proceedings or justify their cultural nationalist struttings, now ninety-three and living in a nursing home. The Queen Mother was reactivated once again, rolled in her wheelchair onto the stage at the Million Man March while someone read her statement of support. Afterward, she was doubtless returned to the nursing home to languish until the men needed her again.

Although I think it was a serious mistake for her to attend the march, at least Dr. Dorothy Height, president of the National Council of Negro Women for forty years, heads a national organization of black women and could honestly claim to represent a constituency, conservative and soft-spoken as it is. The same cannot be said for poet Maya Angelou, who seems to represent only herself, cannot be defined as a leader, and whose recent actions have been destructive to black women. Angelou supported Clarence Thomas's nomination to the Supreme Court. Went to visit ex-heavyweight champion Mike Tyson in prison while serving a sentence for raping an eighteen-year-old black beauty pageant contestant, afterward likened him to Malcolm X, and supported his hero's welcome in Harlem. Maya expectations were already low to nil. Who could be surprised that Angelou, who has made a career and fortune out of her own triumphant victimization and embraced the role of some sort of weird literary Mammy figure, an image comforting to many white folks and non-threateningly inspirational to some black ones, was there? Lights, camera, action, book sales! Here's Maya!

It is not insignificant that the majority of the women invited to the march were post-menopausal. As someone who will herself be post-menopausal sooner than later, let me say I have no problem with menopause. Thirty years of monthly bleeding, PMS, cramps, pregnancy scares, and making the tampon manufacturers rich is enough. I'm not only ready for menopause, I'm looking forward to it. It is not menopause that is problematic, but the way in which society views, and conditions post-menopausal women to view, themselves. Desexualized, no longer feminine, without importance or power, we become less than women, since in the eyes of men women's power derives from our sexuality and ability to procreate. Post-menopausal, men no longer feel the need to see, hear, or fear us, we have been made neuter, harmless. As always, the roles for women diverge when race is a factor. If post-menopausal white women ascend and become matrons, black women descend even lower than we already are and become mammies, our function to offer comfort and sustenance, to nurture. Those women who do not go gently into that dark night of menopause, emerging out the other end as desexualized mammy figures are problems, bad girls who will not go along with the male program. No longer able to function as Mommy and have children, and rejecting the role of Mammy, women's usefulness to men is almost nonexistent. The fact that we remain vibrant, intelligent, sexual beings, and that for most women not having to worry about pregnancy is a profoundly liberating experience, is not appreciated. The culture, not knowing what to do with us or how to use us, most often simply ignores us.

There were the chosen few at the Million Man March, buoyant in a sea of testosterone, while the rest of us black women were not invited, were told to stay home and teach the children while the men atoned and bonded, bonded and atoned, as if black women remaining in the community and quietly taking care of business while the men are elsewhere is anything new.

My cynicism toward the women at the Million Man March has nothing to do with sour grapes. Even if black women had been invited to the march, even if Louie Farrakhan had hand-delivered an invitation to my house, even if he'd asked me to deliver the benediction, I wouldn't have gone. When I first heard that there was to be a Million Man March in D.C., I ran to 125th Street and risked death by car crash to buy my issue of the *Final Call*, the newspaper of the Nation of Islam, from a bow-tied brother hawking them in the middle of the street. I read that newspaper more than once and still couldn't figure out what the agenda, the point, of the march was, besides some vague "feel good" exercise for black men.

I heard the rhetoric and liked the notion of black men "atoning" for their often dismal treatment of black women, but I never understood the choice of venue. The Howard Inn, D.C.'s only black hotel, is no longer in business, and the Florida Avenue Grill, Ben's Chili Bowl, and all the rest of the black-owned restaurants in Washington combined couldn't feed a few thousand people, much less a million. Why are a million black men going to pay money to get to Washington, check into hotels and eat in restaurants, where they will spend big bucks primarily with white folks, and then mill around a million strong on property controlled by the most right-wing, wrong-thinking, racist government in recent years, to atone to black women? It also didn't seem fair that black women would be excluded from the spectacle of a million black men figuratively chanting, en masse, "We're sorry, we're sorry, we're sorry," a once-in-a-lifetime event that no sister would want to miss. Even when we're the ones being atoned to, our presence is unnecessary, we remain invisible, nonessential. It's enough that we provide backdrop, our presence is definitely not requested. And what's the logic behind going to the white man to atone to black women, as if going to confession before the great white father, hoping for absolution? Wouldn't it have been more effective for black men to amass in southeast D.C., a neighborhood with one of the highest crime rates in the country, and shut down the crack houses, seize the guns, clean up the community, talk to the young brothers? But that would have required work and ongoing commitment.

Was the atonement really to black women, or was that just a cover story to hide the far more ominous agenda, that black men were going to apologize to the great patriarchal white father for not being real men and keeping their women and children in line, to pledge allegiance to the patriarchy of the United States of America? Finally, there's the obvious, that whatever black men's failings in America, they pale in comparison to what was visited upon all black people by slavery and its continuing aftermath. When it comes to who needs to atone in America, black men are not at the top of the list.

It is impossible not to feel that there is a fearful symmetry between Louis Farrakhan's Nation of Islam, the Promise Keepers, and the Christian Coalition, each of whose analysis of the crisis in American society holds as central the contention that men have abdicated their God-given role, that women and children are out of control, and men need to unite as men and crack the whip, patriarchy as redemption. The rise of the so-called "Christian" right, the

Million Man March, and the recent emergence of men's groups like Promise Keepers, a group led by former football coach Bill McCartney, who by the fall of 1996 had drawn over a million Christian patriarchs to mass meetings, is extremely troubling. On the real side, it's difficult not to suspect that, at least for the leadership of the Million Man March, it was fundamentally about posturing, just another dick thang. But unlike those black thangs, which as the T-shirt states, white folks don't understand, if there's one thing black women recognize blindfolded, it's black men and their dick thing.

I never did find out what the official agenda of the march was. I don't think there was one beyond providing Nation of Islam leader Louis Farrakhan with an international stage on which to speak and allowing black men to feel as if they'd done something, and by extension, better, simply by their presence. But one day of great vibes, brotherly love, not dogging women, and no fighting does not a transformation make, although like many black people I enjoyed hearing Farrakhan lecture the world about white supremacy, speak truth to power. Farrakhan's popularity and black Americans' tragedy is that he's about the only leader who does anymore. Most of them don't even talk bad or sell woof tickets. Black so-called leadership has accepted their consignment to the colored leadership ghetto, where their primary function is to either bemoan or denigrate the state of black people. They are never allowed to critique white people. Even through all the rhetoric and bad politics, Louis Farrakhan speaks to and for a broad spectrum of black folks because he dares to speak some truth, as many black folks see it, to white people, plain and simple. This is what we hear, respond to, and remember, even though most of what he said in his two-hour-plus speech was a lot of mumbo jumbo.

But the truth is, even if there had been a clear agenda beyond atoning to the banished and I'd gotten a personal invitation, I still wouldn't have been there. As a black woman who battles daily to love myself, be visible, and place myself in the center, there is no way for me to go anywhere at the behest of Louis Farrakhan or Ben Chavis. That these two tired usual suspects could summon a million black men to Washington on a Monday morning speaks to three things: black men's desperate desire for leadership, white folks' response to the verdict in the O. J. Simpson trial a few weeks earlier, and the irrelevance of black women.

Much has been said about the vacuum in black leadership, but let's be honest, it's way beyond the vacuum stage, more like a black hole. When it comes to black leadership, there is none. Every time the anchorperson on the news show says the next segment will be a discussion with black leaders, I have no more inkling of whose faces I'll see after the commercial break than the most uninterested white person. These days, "black leaders" seem to be primarily opportunists with the requisite amount of black blood to be visually perceived as black and therefore declared representatives of the race, and those with an uncontrollable desire to be on television and the facility to provide a few quotable sound bites, even if they're wrong and ridiculous. If you do happen to see, hear, or read about a black leader who actually makes sense, does some work, and leads someone, their presence is probably a mistake. They'll be whisked away, seldom, if ever, to reappear. Nowadays, leaders become leaders through media repetition: If they're around enough, they're declared leaders, by themselves or white reporters, only rarely by any black constituency.

Black leaders come in three basic brands. First, there are the political ambulance chasers. These are local Negroes, usually never elected to anything, whose stock in trade appears to be scanning the news for trouble with a possible racial slant, rushing to the scene of the crime, riling people up with tired yet dangerous rhetoric—

often consisting of a contemporary twist of "It's all whitey's fault"—
and preaching to the television cameras. These ambulance chasers
are distinguished by the fact that they have no organization, institution, ongoing agenda, visible means of support (also known as a
job), and don't actually do anything other than run their mouths for
the microphone. If a citizen, hearing them, wanted to join up, they'd
be hard-pressed to find out where: there is no where there once the
cameras are turned off.

Then there are the "black leaders" who are elected to public office as a result of usually minuscule voter turnout and those who
lead black organizations. Often, the major accomplishment of the
elected officials is that they continue to be reelected even as they do
little or nothing for their communities. They are simply, like many
elected officials irrespective of color, hustlers who've managed to
obtain a job for life. Those who lead organizations lead groups that
used to do something for black folks, organizations that are thinking about—maybe—trying to do something for black folks, and
those that do nothing for any black people other than the ones on
their payroll. By and large, both these types of leaders' legitimacy is
derived from longevity, as in, "They've been around for so long and
my grandfather told me they used to be great," or the issuance of
thick annual reports bemoaning the state of black Americans without suggesting, much less effecting, any program for change, or
those based on pure opportunism and mau-mauing of white folks.
An excellent example of this is Roy Innis, the head of CORE (The
Congress on Racial Equality). Innis is a right-wing opportunist,
ideologue, and political pimp known for his apparently boundless
support of reactionaries from New York to Angola. Every year he
raises hundreds of thousands of dollars at a posh dinner in downtown Manhattan in which he gives out so-called "Civil Rights"
awards to a multiracial group composed of those who are rich, con-

nected, and if not politically dangerous as symbols of an acceptably passive notion of liberalism, at best naive.

Finally, there is the cadre of black people who become black leaders because they are incapable of saying no to media requests to pontificate. Like their white counterparts, they are called pundits. In blackface they come in two basic varieties. First, there are blackfaces that are recognizable, famous, possessors of celebrity status. One can almost hear the television producers in the studio in the midst of booking that evening's guests for a program on nuclear disarmament shouting to his youthful minions, "Get a nuclear physicist from MIT, a representative of an anti-nuclear group, an environmentalist, and, oh, yeah, see if you can get Spike Lee or another black!" Since most black people don't exist in the minds of most white Americans as anything but predators and criminals, it'll be someone famous, for what doesn't matter. Still, there are requirements within the parameters of "generic famous black" too. That person should definitely be male, and in the best of all possible worlds a neo-conservative whose basic analysis consists of the wholesale promotion of America, cheering rugged individualism, and laying the blame for whatever the problem is at the feet of the colored population. Particularly popular are black men who scoff at the existence of racism, present their own success as examples of the existence of a meritocracy in a non-racist culture, and urge black people to "Stop Whining" about racism and pull themselves up by their bootstraps. Hey, that kind of subterfuge got Clarence Thomas onto the Supreme Court, it can damned sure get a few of us on "Meet the Press."

To be black and a pundit is to be part of a catch-all, jack of all trades and master of none, or at least usually not the one you're asked to pontificate on. This group includes all ilk of black leaders, from ambulance chasers to elected officials to heads of organizations that actually have a membership, to heads of organizations with "Black" or "Equality" or "Civil Rights" in the title, of which the only member is yourself, and anyone else with a recognizable name, face, and the yen to go on television. Occasionally, a pundit will appear who actually does something and has something to say, but they are few and far between. As often as not, the best black folks can expect from these pundit-leaders is the Reverend Jesse Jackson. It should be noted that as Jackson's political ascendancy has plummeted from the highs of his presidential runs in 1984 and 1988, so has the power, influence, and resonance of his punditry. Nowadays, as often as not there is something kind of sad about Jackson the pundit, as if underneath his suit and tie he's wearing a T-shirt emblazoned with the words "I Coulda Been a Contender." But this does not matter. The objective of punditry is to become a pundit for all seasons, any reason, like Stanley Crouch or Armstrong Williams since the real objective isn't to say anything important but to advertise whatever it is you're selling, books, movies, or self.

When it comes to black leadership in any form, black women are invisible, except in cases of extreme emergency. California Congresswoman Maxine Waters got some play in the spring of 1993, but that was only after the acquittal of the four L.A. police officers accused of beating Rodney King and millions of dollars' worth of damage caused by the subsequent rebellions. Waters got to be a leader for a moment because she was unavoidable: she represents South Central L.A., where most of the action took place. But almost as soon as CNN stopped broadcasting its live images of out-of-control colored people, Waters disappeared. No matter that she actually does work, is smart, eloquent, and has solutions. Once the fires stopped burning, Waters disappeared, replaced by the same old bankrupt black male leaders and their white counterparts.

Louis Farrakhan and Ben Chavis are prominent links in a long line of tired black leaders. Perhaps the only thing new about them is the level of their public contempt for women. As head of the NAACP, Ben Chavis was accused of sexually harassing a woman who worked with him, and when she threatened to file suit he tried to use the NAACP's money—more than a quarter million dollars of it—to shut her up. Louis Farrakhan, leader of the patriarchal Nation of Islam, has a long history of chauvinist behavior, but what sticks in my mind is a speech he gave during the rape trial of Mike Tyson, during which he minced and squealed in a vicious imitation of Desiree Washington, Tyson's victim, suggesting that Tyson's behavior was her fault, that for a young woman to be alone in his presence was the equivalent of "letting a fox into the hen house" and that the hen got what she deserved.

It is not by coincidence that both Chavis and Farrakhan are preachers. The religious community is the most popular pool from which black leaders spring. It is of little consequence that one is Christian, the other Muslim, since the bonds of ego, opportunism, and patriarchy are sometimes capable of erasing even religious differences. (At press time, Chavis said he had embraced Allah. Stay tuned.) Both are masters of rhetoric and the use of religious symbols and references that black Americans, the people more Christian than those who invented Christianity, fall for every time. Both lead constituencies of dubious size in which the one sure thing is that black women are doing most of the work, getting little or none of the credit, and silent. If black women decided to boycott black religious institutions for a week, they'd cease to function. Instead we continue to worship faithfully, tithe, answer the telephone, and cook the minister's lunch. In exchange we get a promise of heaven in the hereafter while the men chow down on the pieces of heaven on earth we've served up.

It is unacceptable for black women or black men to accept as leaders men incapable of respecting and treating women, and the issues that affect us specifically because of our gender, as equals. On the issue of women, both Farrakhan and Chavis are black men for whom the objective is to get a piece of the pie. It is not to eliminate male dominance, but simply to position themselves as more benevolent patriarchs, a contradiction in terms as far as I'm concerned. For them, it is not the dominance of men that is bad, but the dominance of bad—and for them this means white—men. They're not troubled by the oppression of women by men, they just want a piece of the action. There's lots of room for agreement between Ben and Louis, they're more alike than different, although one suspects that Farrakhan, married for forty-two years to the same woman and the father of nine children and grandfather of twenty-two, might be a bit chagrined by Chavis's reputed sexual behavior. But maybe that's not a very important difference anyway. Farrakhan's spiritual leader and founder of the Nation of Islam, the Honorable Elijah Muhammed (from whom Malcolm X broke toward the end of his life, devastated by the contradiction between Muhammed's words and his deeds), was himself a serial fornicator who fathered thirteen children by seven women out of wedlock. In a way, all of the above begs the simple question. Where have Farrakhan, Chavis, or most of these other leaders actually led us? What have they done that has challenged the U.S. government? Demonstrably changed the existence of substantial numbers of black people, black communities, black children?

The truth is that neither Farrakhan nor Chavis by themselves has the juice to bring a million men to Washington. That was left to those with the real juice, O. J. Simpson and White Folks. If it wasn't a godsend, Allah the beneficent and merciful in action, it was certainly fortuitous for the organizers of the Million Man March that the not guilty verdict in the trial of O. J. Simpson came on October 3, a scant two weeks before the march. Rumors abounded that O. J. planned to attend as Grand Marshall and that defense attorney Johnnie Cochran would ride in on a float, designed to be a facsimile of a slave ship. But it was not the acquittal of Simpson that provided added impetus for hundreds of thousands of black men to go to Washington. It was white folks' response to that acquittal.

In 1989, when five black teenagers were arrested and accused of the brutal rape and beating of a white woman jogger in New York's Central Park, news reports described the youths as having stumbled upon her while out "wilding." Born black and living in a black community, I'd never heard the term "wilding" before, and neither had anyone else I asked. But the media was quick to define us to us and tell the world that "wilding" was a popular sport in our communities, consisting of bands of young sociopaths roaming the streets on the lookout for someone to victimize. (One explanation of the term is that a reporter misheard a youth's explanation of what the young men were doing in the park, which he described as "the wild thing," the phrase taken from the 1988 hit song by Los Angeles rapper Tone Loc, "Wild Thing." So much for journalistic accuracy.) Whatever its origins, the previously unknown pastime of "wilding," the random victimization and brutalization of one by many, entered the cultural vocabulary.

The response of most white Americans to Simpson's acquittal put to rest the notion that wilding was a black thing. On hearing the not guilty verdict, white America went about its own form of wilding, intellectually and politically trying to destroy or discredit any and every black person who either thought O. J. was innocent or was glad he was acquitted, never understanding that these were often not the same thing. The jury, composed predominantly of black women, was dismissed as stupid, incompetent, and racist. The jury system, with its requirement of unanimity in verdicts, was condemned and arguments were made to change the law so that ten, or six, or two, or however many guilty votes were available, could result in a conviction. The acquittal of O. J. Simpson, a famous and rich man who is estimated to have spent six million dollars on his defense, was widely interpreted as sounding the death knell for the American system of jurisprudence and opening the doors for black men's unrestrained victimization of white women, in short, shaking the very foundations of America as white folks know and love it. The Republic was threatened! Extreme measures were demanded! No mention was made of the fact that on the day Simpson received his multimillion-dollar, celebrity-drenched acquittal, thousands of black men, some of whom were actually innocent, were convicted and sent to prison across America.

More than any amount of organizing done by Louis, Ben, or their minions, it was the Simpson verdict—and white folks' wilding response to it as articulated by pundits, experts, and the man and woman in the street—that was instrumental in bringing hundreds of thousands of men to the Million Man March. Will white people never understand that part of the mentality of black folks in America, and any oppressed people anywhere, is the knowledge that often that which the dominant culture condemns most vociferously is also that which is potentially most beneficial to us? Even if, like the Million Man March, its long-range benefits are vague and elusive, the short-term value of amassing a million black men on the mall is obvious. If nothing else, it's like giving the collective finger to white folks, and in their own front yard. It's ironic that the impetus for bringing more black people together to demonstrate since the 1963 March on Washington was O. J. Simpson, who has repeatedly said that he doesn't want to be viewed as black, but simply as a man, and whose connection and allegiance to the black community over the last three decades has been, at best, an accident of birth.

I enjoy messing with white folks' racism, selling woof tickets, and grand spectacle as much as the next person, but ultimately I do not see how black women benefited from any of it. Not the presence of the widows and role models, or the rhetoric of black leaders, or the acquittal of O. J. Simpson, or the Million Man March. All of them seem to further marginalize and erase us, which made it all the more heartbreaking to see Rosa Parks and Betty Shabazz and Queen Mother Moore and Maya Angelou on stage at the march, reminding us of their own and all black women's ongoing erasure by their brief appearances. While I'm sure each woman had individual reasons for being there, it is not enough. What was missing is a sense of collectivity, an understanding of the impact their presence, and by their presence putting the black woman's seal of approval on the event, had on all of us. Just as the men in D.C. on October 16 came to symbolize all black men in America, so did the few black women allowed brief voice. They became, whether they meant to or we liked it, officially sanctioned representatives of African American women, giving our female blessing to a march led by corrupt, misogynistic wolves in preachers' clothing.

Probably half of the men I know, like, and love went to the march. They went because they felt hopeless. Because they are already working or want to work for social change. Because they're frustrated. They went because at least it was something for black men to do, and maybe, just maybe, something good and enduring would come of it. These men, and most of the other men who were there, were either working or middle class. Men who took a day off from the transit authority, or the practice of law, or teaching, or the post office, or being artists, from some job, who went into their pockets and paid money to go to Washington. The good, decent, hardworking men. The tragedy is that those most in need of help, the true predators, the violent, the tackheads and ignoramuses, the woman beaters, child abandoners, and refuse-to-workniks, the ones who most need to get themselves together, were largely absent. Significantly, the march was peopled by black men who in society's eyes have made it, but remain angry, frustrated, in despair. The good Negroes. Forget what was said during the speechifying by Farrakhan and others, the real message came from the very presence of hundreds of thousands of working- and middle-class men. Testimony to the enduring and most probably permanent nature of racism in this culture.

I kept the television on most of the day, listening more than watching. I found it hard to sit still and view the spectacle. To do so would have been to forget who I was, actively collude in my own erasure. I was profoundly disturbed by the notion that black men can transform themselves or this culture absent black women. The whole day was an assault on my sensibilities, one that made me feel vulnerable, threatened, in some vague way afraid to go outside. The exclusion of black women and focus on black men standing up and taking back control of their women and children reminded me of a line in Ntozake Shange's *for colored girls* . . . "Somebody almost walked off wid alla my stuff . . ." I will not stand for this theft of sisters' collective labor in churches, public schools, unions, community organizations, in our families. How to resist it then, when we are without self-selected leadership, without voice? Who speaks for us?

Certainly not Coretta Scott King, widow of Martin Luther King, Jr., who did not attend the march, and Betty Shabazz, widow of Malcolm X, who did. Both women are often projected as leaders and spokespeople for black women. Both have played the role of one who is seen and seldom heard, to the hilt. Without diminishing the suffering and sacrifices of either of their lives, the fact is that their visibility, power, and ascendance as role models, spokeswomen, or any other public function, is solely predicated on the men they married. As widows, the power they receive is by proxy. They do not in their own right represent important ideas, or commitments, or activism. Rather, they have panache, juice, usefulness, by association. That they were married to great men does not mean that therefore they are great women. For black men looking for someone to pimp for their own purposes, what this means is that maybe there is some residue of his greatness left on her, the afterglow of intimate association with power, that they can capitalize on. Invisible and silent until their husband's murders, martyrdom, and their dignified ascension to widowhood, the culture has frozen them in that moment, confined them to a purgatory on earth where their lives are subverted to the memory of their husbands, and the use others wish those memories to serve. They become professional widows.

Not a gig anyone in their right mind would choose, but not such a bad one if you're Jacqueline Kennedy Onassis, widow of President John F. Kennedy, or Ethel Kennedy, widow of Senator Robert F. Kennedy. In short, if you're white. Being rich doesn't hurt at all. Jackie O and Ethel K were immediately embraced and protected by America following their husbands' assassinations. Pregnant when RFK was killed, Ethel Kennedy became the quintessential Mother: all-giving and all-suffering. Jackie became the ultimate culture maven, responsible, as some pundits put it, for teaching Americans about culture, style, and grace. No matter that both men had their heads blown open right here, in America, land of the free and home of the brave. Once dispatched to the other side, JFK and RFK became martyrs and their widows received the posthumous perks. No such luck for Coretta and Betty, lush widowhood and iconicity being something reserved for white widows. As JFK said, life isn't fair. When you're black in America death isn't fair, either.

Widowed, Coretta and Betty were left to scuffle to support their children, themselves, live decent lives as best they could. Of the two, Coretta's economic road has been easier because King's politics and presence were less overtly frightening than Malcolm's. But the price of support for his widow has been the transformation of King from a visionary activist into a non-threatening dreamer. The man must be spinning in his grave at having been deconstructed into merely a "man who had a dream" and commodified into a national holiday complete with department stores advertising their "Martin Luther King, Jr. Day White Sale! Sheets 25% to 50% Off!" You'd think the only speech King ever made was at the March on Washington in 1963; "I have a dream, I have a dream, I have a dream" is all you hear. This transformation of King into a dreamer and commodity serves to ignore his activism, distort his accomplishments, and diminish his tremendous intellect. It also conveniently ignores King's understanding and advocacy toward the end of his life of the importance of class as well as race, his emphasis on poor people, and his anti-war activism. The establishment and funding of The King Center in Atlanta, under Coretta's leadership, promulgates the myth that we love Martin, accept his ideals, when nothing could be further from the truth.

Society's refusal to confer on Betty Shabazz even a subsistence level of perks for professional widowhood speaks profoundly to how we felt, and feel, about Malcolm X. Unable to so easily commodify and neuter the wicked-tongued and uncompromising Malcolm X, Betty Shabazz has had a rougher row to hoe. She returned to school, got her doctorate, and now works at a regular job. Malcolm is not exactly good material for cooptation, the primary motive for support of the widows. It is only recently, nearly thirty years after his death, that the commodification and neutralization of Malcolm X has gotten into full swing, in large part as a result of the popularization of Malcolm in Spike Lee's 1992 film, *Malcolm X*. With all the Malcolm X-abilia on the market, you'd think he was Mr. Popular while he lived, that most black people actively supported him—we didn't—and that the only thing the man ever said was "By any means necessary," over and over, like a skip in an old record.

The culture's support of widows and commodification of their husbands is inextricably linked to the services that support purchases: Jackie O's style bolsters the myth of JFK's Camelot, washes away his escalation of the war in Vietnam, his cowardly avoidance of civil rights, his personal failures. Ethel's ascendance as Every Mom, mother of eleven(!), allows us as a nation not to feel so bad that we created a place where people get their heads blown off after winning the California primary. The extent to which Coretta and Betty have enjoyed this support is dependent upon the culture's need to control and direct the impact the life and words of a Martin or Malcolm could have today, particularly on young people, who face lives far more hopeless than we could have imagined thirty years ago.

What dismal options. We can either front for black men, be professional widows, or, occasionally, emergency pundits. But sometimes for black women, visibility for whatever purpose and at any cost beats a blank. It also helps pay the bills. Without an infrastructure to support the heirs of martyrs to American racism, the black community offers them few alternatives other than to create a cottage industry based on the past achievements of the woman's husband. It is not enough. The burning of Betty Shabazz makes clear the need for the black community to provide economic, emotional and psychological support not only to the widows but their children and grandchildren.

One has no idea who these women are, or what they might

have become, had their husbands lived. For all we know, they might have divorced, raised their children as single parents, become brain surgeons, beaten Mae Jemison to become the first black woman in space. Maybe they would have lived happily ever after according to our notion of what this means, but reality indicates that's unlikely. We'll never know. What we do know is that our society is more comfortable with the static image of the dignified, grieving widow silently accepting her bereavement than with real live women who speak up and rock the boat. If you doubt it, think about the incredulous, dismissive response to Coretta when she spoke up and demanded a trial for James Earl Ray in early 1997, almost thirty years after her husband's assassination. Instead of being able to live their lives, both Coretta and Betty are frozen in time and yet still alive, a cybergenic experiment gone bust. Eternally static because of their widowhood, they are dragged from decade to decade, timeless icons for all black women, forever, seldom individuated in their own right.

Black women's silence in the face of the selection and projection of Coretta, Betty, Maya, Queen Mother Moore, and a few others as sterling examples of black womanhood, role models, if you will, is, as silence often is, acquiescence. By neither critiquing nor rejecting these male-selected role models, we also fail to become or push forth as alternatives activist women with voices. We tacitly accept not only male control of our leaders are and what our concerns are, but the representatives of black women in public leadership as anachronistic, passive, desexualized beings often distinguished largely by their subservient relationship to great men or their male-centered politics. I have never known, seen, met, heard of, or read a black woman who described these women—with the possible exception of Rosa Parks—as her role model. By the same token, I'd be hard-pressed to find more than a handful of black women willing to publicly critique their projection as such. The absence of empowered black women as public voices is not as disturbing as the fact that we seem too beaten down, brainwashed, selfish, or self-hating to do anything about it. Even as we listened to Maya read yet another poem, watched Queen Mother Moore being pimped by the Nation of Islam, saw Betty Shabazz ally herself with a man she has publicly implied she believes was involved in her husband's assassination, we said nothing publicly. Of course, the telephone lines of many sisters burned that day as we created a web of our anger, disgust, and sorrow. For many black women, watching the Million Man March on television was a collective experience. As separated and silent as we are, we all felt something. For me, in addition to Farrakhan, Chavis, no agenda, the no invite thing, the dick thing, the patriarchal thing, the march's decision to exclude black women as a group and then to include a select few who they deemed acceptable representatives was devastating. Men deciding who among us are the officially designated representatives of grown-up black women.

Across age and class, most black women who were uncomfortable with the march declined to say so publicly. I was one of them. At the time, I chose not to participate in that battle for reasons that seemed pragmatic: I was involved in organizing work focused on women and didn't want to get distracted by an estrogen vs. testosterone battle over the march; I didn't want to be used to represent white people's disdain for Farrakhan and the march by the media; I calculated that if I stayed out of this one, the men would have to be supportive on issues important to black women. Good reasons, but still excuses. There is no denying that I am painfully aware of the price a black woman pays when she publicly disagrees with black men, and didn't want to pay it for the Million Man March.

Some women turned their discomfort into a cynical kind of

support, summed up by that old saying, "Do something, even if it's wrong." Their rationale was essentially that black men are so messed up they were willing to sacrifice themselves on the altar of helping the poor, pitiful brothers get it together. Black men who participated in the march evidenced the same low expectations, most tellingly in the frequently heard comment, "It was wonderful to have so many black men together and there was no fighting." Talk about damning with faint praise.

It was easy for me to choose silence. I love black men, in the particular and the abstract, too much to offer them such grudging, contemptuous, condescending support, as if they are incapable of doing right, genetically predisposed to do nothing, and so should be encouraged and patted on the head whatever they do in an effort to get it together, even if it is at my expense. I love myself too much for that.

But the larger question has nothing to do with the march, but with us. Why are we unorganized and silent, and what can we do about it? Sometimes I think black women have gone so long without reflection that we no longer look for one. Sometimes I think we are so parched for images of ourselves that any one will do. I am afraid that we are so used to being invisible, without image or voice, that we have lost the ability to imagine ourselves and people like us. Once in my lifetime, a movie like *Waiting to Exhale* comes along, and black women flock to theaters, happy to see black women on screen, larger than life. Even though they are not real, we embrace them because they are at least the skeletons of who we would like to be, visible black women with voice. Then the screen goes dark and we return to our world, where we all know the price black women pay for speaking out. Social isolation. Verbal and psychological attack. Physical brutalization. Economic and political ostracism. Further marginalization by a culture in which we already hang by a thread.

The truth is that even when we obey, keep our mouths shut, wait to be seen and heard until the men ask us, black women remain excluded. The women at the Million Man March did not represent us for many reasons, the most important being that it is unacceptable for black men—or anyone other than black women—to choose who represents black women. Ever. Under any conditions. Black women are best represented by those of us who were unseen, known and unknown, those who supported the march and those who did not. By the sister at the library on 125th Street, a clutch of children in tow, who scoffed when I asked her what she thought of the march. "Think?" she echoed. "I don't think anything. I've got too much work to do to spend time thinking about that."

It is the responsibility of those of us who are trying to become and live our lives as grown-up black women to communicate what that means and entails to other women. But we cannot offer younger women new ways to look at themselves if we have not devised them for ourselves. An essential part of what happens when women begin to come together and talk about themselves is the emergence of a common, collective vision of who we are. We need to stop lying, self-deluding, competing with each other, and fronting and honestly examine our real lives as women: our secondary status, the political, economic, and sometimes personal violence we live with, the aspirations we have that are so often subsumed by the needs of others. We need to tell younger women the truth about our pain, powerlessness, and silence. If we do this we can begin to develop new ideas of what it means to be a black woman, definitions that are expansive and will engage all of us. This is one of the ways we can build a community of black women, one with common experiences, concerns, and a collective agenda. Then we can begin to talk about the future possibilities for ourselves and those women who follow us. Until then, we will remain reactionary, responding to what men and the larger society do to, say about, or expect of us. For this to change we have to acknowledge that we are in crisis, declare ourselves important, and start talking about where we want to go. Each of us needs to ask ourselves, "What do you plan to be doing and who do you want to be five years from now?" In this way we begin to define goals and think strategically, develop a vision of self and the future. The alternative is to continue to accept powerlessness and fight for the crumbs others occasionally toss us. To abdicate our role as mothers, daughters, sisters, aunts, and grandmothers. To simply drift along in life, without direction or vision, acceding through our silence and passivity to both white racist pronouncements and blackface patriarchal visions of who we are and what our roles—and who our role models—should be.

Self-definition is not an easy task under any circumstances. It is more difficult when you are without support or reflection, absent accessible images of women who act, have voice, and wield power. Other than occasional visibility conferred on "safe" black women, or a sister who, like Anita Hill, Maxine Waters, or Lani Guinier, appears briefly in the midst of crisis, or the fleeting and dubious power of our sexuality that makes us desirable to men, we are most often unseen. I agree with Elaine Brown, former head of the Black Panther Party and author of the autobiography *A Taste of Power,* that too often black women's power is reduced to what Brown calls the "power of the pussy. You could withhold it, or give it to manipulate men to act. That's a sad comment on life, isn't it?" What is critical is that black women begin to place ourselves, our issues, and our voices in the center of the debate, not only about women and black people, but about all the critical issues in the culture. It is a fallacy to believe or accept that black women or black people live outside American society, basically unaffected by what goes on except when the subject is race. The alternative is to consign ourselves to be unseen and unheard until someone else, usually male, finds some use for us, and you can bet your bottom dollar whatever their use for us, it'll be of little or no use to us.

There are mirrors scattered in odd places around my house. I catch my reflection tying my shoes, reading in my favorite chair, turning a corner. There are pictures of black women I like tucked in unexpected places too. Fannie Lou Hamer, Joycelyn Elders, Dinah Washington, Maxine Waters, Aretha, Winnie Mandela, Sarah Vaughan, Queen Latifah, Harriet Tubman, Cassandra Wilson, Myrlie Evers, women I know and women I never met whose strength and sense of self is abundant. These mirrors and pictures remind me that I, we, exist, and of all the magnificent things we have done and can do. A black woman's custom-made funhouse of affirmation. They help sustain me when I leave the house every day, just another barely visible sister who, as Mississippi activist Fannie Lou Hamer said, is sick and tired of being sick and tired, fighting against erasure, for voice and respect.

THE NIGGERBITCHFIT

THERE IS BETWEEN BLACK WOMEN a language all our own, sometimes spoken, oftentimes not. We communicate with each other through a tilt of our head, a quick cutting of eyes, a heartfelt exhalation of breath as we pass in the street, a quiet sucking of teeth, a fleeting smile that can absolutely transform the tenor of a bad day.

It is a feminine, coded, unwritten language that cuts many ways. It is complex in its simplicity, as were the languages created by slaves denied the use of their native tongue but compelled to communicate. Black women's language grows out of our particular experience of oppression because of our race and our gender. Each gesture and word has multiple, sometimes contradictory meanings. It is a language that transcends class, age, skin tone, attitude, cuts to the essential chase of our femaleness.

Some of this language black men share with us. That is the part

that has to do with racism and white people. We are skilled at saying what is acceptable to the dominant group while at the same time
saying what we mean to one another. We have had centuries to
practice dissembling, shucking, and jiving, making white people
feel comfortable and unthreatened even as we deceive, laugh at, and
conspire against them. But there is a part of the language that only
black women speak and understand, and it is that part which is in-
extricable from our being women. We use this language to discuss
what is our business: our bodies, minds, hearts, dreams, children,
rage, and joy. That business often involves men, the wonderful and
heartbreaking quality of our interaction with them, the ways in
which we are treated at home, in the streets, in the bedroom, in our
communities, in the world.

Most of the time no one but us hears or notices when we speak
our language, it is a surreptitious, quiet dialect, this dialogue among
women. Crossing a street on the way to work early in the morning,
a man in a four-wheel-drive vehicle wants to turn right, but we are
crossing the street, black women, some with children in tow, drop-
ping them off at school on our way to the job. He does not allow
us the right of way, but turns rapidly in front of us so that we must
stop or be run over. A sister turns toward me and cuts her eyes, I
suck my teeth, behind me a woman mutters, "Typical!," in seconds
the eight of us in the crosswalk connect, acknowledge the man's lack
of courtesy, pass judgment. All the while we keep stepping toward
the curb, reach it, and scatter in various directions. "You all have a
nice day," a woman singsongs, and each of us laughs, nods, briefly
united by her affirmation of his blindness and of our visibility, her
positive wish.

We speak this language numerous times each day, casually, without thinking, noticing, never having to fumble for the right word or
syntax as we do with languages consciously learned. I do not know

if we were born knowing this language, but do know that it is absorbed early in the company of mothers, sisters, aunts, grandmothers, other women. Heard as a little girl in the shift of lap or shoulder when men, or white people, or those who are not like us come around, seen in the movement of eyes, heads, legs, the two- or three-word comments that elicit that black woman's head-tilting thing, or smiles or frowns or gales of womanly laughter when they exit.

Created out of a need to communicate rapidly and secretly, mostly this language is abbreviated, quiet, its words and gestures so rich that a few suffice. This is as it must be, because most of the time black women are too busy taking care of others to take time to care for ourselves and one another. We communicate in passing, on the way someplace more important than where we are, about events great and small. The body language and movements of my sisters tell me what they feel about the night before, the weather, the everyday violence we all encounter, local and national politics, their own lives.

Sometimes, usually under extreme and negative circumstances, our women's language mutates, a woman's voice expands, grows loud, broadens so that everyone who hears her knows, if not exactly what she's talking about, then at least her rage. In these moments, we tell our secrets, let the cat out of the bag. Mostly, this happens individually, when one woman has reached her end, has had enough of violence, or dishonesty, or being demonized, or being invisible, and breaks out, goes off. It is a powerful thing when this happens. Imagine how much power we'd have as black women if we could figure out how to do this collectively.

One day I'm talking to my friend the writer Thulani Davis on the telephone, we are both nearing the end of the rope in our work, that point at which we either cut ourselves down like Marie

Thompson or hang, and Thulani drawls, "I think maybe it's time to go into my editor's office and have a niggerbitchfit."

And I say, laughing, "A what?"

"Nigger. Bitch. Fit." She enunciates slowly and clearly, so that I will make no mistake. She explains that a niggerbitchfit is what happens when a nice colored girl, having exhausted all possibility of compromise, communication, and peaceful conflict resolution, turns into everyone's worst nightmare, a visible grown-up black woman mad as hell and with nothing to lose, and opens her mouth. When she breaks it down, I am a happy African American woman. The coining of "niggerbitchfit" does two things. It gives name and context to the feelings of anger and rage that for much of my life I'd been taught to deny as antithetical to my conditioning as both a woman and a black woman. If there is one thing women learn early on, it is that anger is unattractive, unladylike, and unacceptable. As black people we are also told early that our rage is always inappropriate. To embrace the concept of the niggerbitchfit shatters a lifetime of conditioning as all-suffering-salt-of-the-earth-stoic-black-woman. It allows me to shed years of explanation and dismissal of my rage as simply being out of control, a manifestation of my penchant for high drama, or just another annoying example of black people's collective chip on our shoulders. With the articulation of the word niggerbitchfit, Thulani let me know not only that my rage was acceptable, but, most important, that I was not alone.

A niggerbitchfit is a combination of a moment of absolute clarity, a psychotic episode, and a revolutionary action. It is an expression of rage out of control, the verbal rejection of the ever-accumulating invisibility, disrespect, and attack from all fronts that is a central part of what it means to be a black woman in America. It is finally voicing what you really think after an extended period of being reasonable, understanding, flexible, pleasant, a team player, a well-behaved colored woman, of going along to get along in a dying white culture and a very unhealthy black one that negates or minimizes our existence moment to moment. It is a frightening thing to experience for those on the receiving end, as its name connotes.

A niggerbitchfit is when the rage of a previously invisible, ignored, or apparently harmless, unimportant, or powerless black woman explodes outward and she transforms herself into a threatening, complaining, out-of-control person, and has a public fit. Niggerbitchfits occur when a sister abruptly realizes that all the good home training our parents gave us, the lessons about working hard, keeping our chin up, standing by our man, being a superwoman, always behaving with dignity, assuming the lifelong mantle of constantly proving to white folks that we're as good as them by being better—as if so-called white people all spring from some Caucasian fountain of goodness and everyone else had best hope we get splashed—doesn't work. It's the adult equivalent of the tantrums children have when they realize the other kids in the game have been cheating, and winning. It's the decision to fight fire with fire.

Most often, black women have our niggerbitchfits alone, in the privacy of our homes, by ourselves. We turn our rage inward and wreak it on ourselves; we drink too much, eat too much, inhale drugs in an effort to beat back the pain and rage. Sometimes, we go verbally or physically off on our children, beat out our frustration on them with open hands or sharp words. Other times we explode on our partners and families, our rage sweeps through the rooms we live in like a tornado and ignites the also building rage of those around us, often to brutal and devastating effect. Those around us hold their breath, shudder, huddle until the fury subsides. Afterward, most often, things go back to what's called normal. All the conditions that created the pressure that created the rage that spawned the niggerbitchfit fall back into place, begin building until the next explosion.

Infrequently, we have a public, collective niggerbitchfit, take our rage and impatience outside ourselves, hurl it strategically, at those responsible for its existence. These are the niggerbitchfits' finest hours, cast in the face of racist or sexist elected officials, or brutal cops, or supervisors who respect neither us nor our work, or boy-men who sell crack to kiddies, or men who refuse to respect women's rights. At its best it is a tool for uniting, organizing, channeling rage into collective power, and that collective power into the ability to effect change. At worst the niggerbitchfit is just another slow way to inflict damage, pain, and death on ourselves and one another.

I have discovered that there is a way to turn my rage into something positive, that it is possible to manage my anger, to turn it to good effect. For years I did not suspect this was possible. I took my anger as proof that there was something wrong with me, that I was a failure as a woman, and a failure as an exemplary black woman, because I felt so much anger, could not figure out how to get rid of it. To deal with my rage, I made her into a separate presence in my life, she became one of my alter egos, a distinct persona who shared, and sometimes invaded, my body and mind. I think many women do this. Often as we go through our days, full as they are with personal, political, and casual violence, we do what we think of as talk to ourselves. We remind ourselves to choose our battles, or calm down, or not go there and get our blood pressure up, or we count to ten. I think, though, that it is not ourselves we talk to, soothe, and admonish in these moments, but that part of ourselves that is our rage. Most often as women we deny our rage, attempt to pacify it, tamp it down and achieve temporary relief, but like the lyrics of a song heard years ago, it stays with us, does not go away. My rage is often so tangible I can have a conversation with it.

"Honey, you had better wake up, get out of the bed, and deal with me!" the familiar voice yells. I pull the covers up over my head, burrow down into the mattress, try to dive into a pleasurable dream, but at this point I'd settle for a nightmare, anything to avoid that grating, relentless, all-too-familiar voice.

"Sorry, darling, won't work, I know that ploy, used to use it myself until I faced the fact there's no escape, ain't nothin' to it but to do, up and at 'em, and all that mess. Jesus, look at your schedule, we have got a full plate, haven't we? The global situation, the national situation, your family situation, your social situation, although that's so slim it's probably overstating the case to even call it a situation, but, as you love to say, hope springs eternal. Oh well. To continue: We've got the political, economic, psychic situation. The newspapers, radio, television, books, the possibilities are endless, there's so much to set us off and so little time. Really, damn near anything is good enough for me as long as there's plenty of it. I'm like an insect that eats twice its own weight every day, or are those birds? Who knows? Who cares? What I do know is I'm hungry. I need to be fed!"

"Get your own food," I mutter.

"Now you know that's impossible. I can't. I'm your dependent, or should I say I'm the enabled and you're my enabler, we're co-dependents, in the lingo of recovery. Or did I pick that up during one of your bouts of shrinkage? Whatever. What's that serenity prayer thing? God grant me the serenity to accept the things I cannot change, the courage to change the things I can, and the wisdom to know the difference . . . Anyway, I'm not just going to shut up and go away and you can't make me, well, that's not true, technically you could, if you knew how, but you don't."

"What do you want to eat?" I ask.

"Oh shit, get up and let's see what's available, after all, life is a smorgasbord full of possibilities, especially for me, sweetheart, the choices are just endless."

"You think so?"

"I know so! Hell, we got war, famine, pestilence, genocide, racism, sexism, classicism, all those other delectable isms. Thank God you go to the gym or we'd get fat." The voice snickers. Fat is a delicate subject with us.

"I don't go to the gym because of my weight!"

"I know, I know, you used to be chunky—that's big in the African American lexicon—but you're not anymore, and I commend you. I know the line 'I go to the gym to deal with my rage, channel it into something constructive, blah, blah, blah,' I've heard it enough. Okay, okay, so I'm temporarily channeled, but temporary is the operative word. Because when you wake up in the morning it's still you and me, baby, and I'm hungry!"

I toss the covers off my face, rub sleep from my eyes, open them. I am alone. I lie there, stretch my arms and legs, sun streams in the window. I rise from the bed to go to the bathroom and my rage, wide awake, unseen but ever present, goes with me. I wait for my water to boil, flick on the television.

"OOOhhh, Bryant Gumbo. I like him, that is a good-looking black man, maybe a little plump in the face, but who's perfect?" my rage says.

"You need to stop emphasizing the superficial and listen to what the man's saying, he is a smart brother," I interrupt.

"Yeah, yeah, smart, smart, smart," Rage snaps. "But let's be honest, sister, do you really care if the man you wake up to first thing in the morning is smart? That is not what you're concerned with, or if you are, it's only if he thinks with his dick!"

"You are so base," I snap. "You couldn't appreciate Bryant Gumbel if your life depended on it."

"Ha!" My rage smirks. "Depends what you mean by appreciate. That Bryant Gumbo . . ."

"Gumbel. It's Gumbel," I interrupt.

"Gumbel, Gumbo, Gummy, who cares? Turn to CNN so I can eat!" my rage commands. I obey. Once fed, my rage quiets.

I am a forty-four-year-old African American woman living in the United States and I have come to understand and accept that my rage is always with me, often you cannot tell us apart, and that is as it must be, we are made for and from each other. Sometimes I forget that my rage is there, but not for long. This becomes increasingly difficult as I get older. My rage feeds off the negativity of the culture that I live in, grows strong, bold, and vociferous every time I read a newspaper, catch a glimpse of Clarence Thomas, an advertisement for Ivory soap, a taxi cab passes me by, hear a rapper singing about bitches and hos, pick up the telephone and hear one of my sisters' wail of pain, read the latest pseudo-scientific mumbo jumbo about the genetic inferiority of black folks, hear the words "welfare reform," remember Deletha Word, imagine all the women like her whose names, faces, and stories I'll never know. Every time a man disrespects me, every time I see another black woman with blonde hair and extensions settling for momentary visibility and no power, every time someone asks me to do something because I'm a woman, my rage grows. Each day I speak up for myself and my sisters and become a highly visible and offensive niggerbitch, every time I refuse to stand behind my man but insist on standing beside him, leading him when necessary, or, like Harriet Tubman, if he isn't willing to fight for freedom leaving him behind, my rage is fed and focused. The credo of my rage is taken from the civil rights song; it goes, "Move on over or I'll move on over you." There is no way for me to stay alive, a black woman in this culture, and not feed my rage. Fed regularly, my rage grows stronger, wiser, more cunning.

My rage is always present, never late, short, or full of maybes, my rage, like Papa, don't take no mess. My rage says nothing to me but yes! yes! yes! And why not? What a host she has found in me, in this nation, in this moment, what better feeding ground for my rage than right here, with me, a black woman existing in a culture that despises women and black people most of all. I am a two-fer in American hell. I have no intention of burning silently.

Once I flirted with being seduced by the culture, bought in, briefly became a part of the corporate American success story, assimilated. It didn't feel right, even though it looked perfect, and after all, facade is substance around these parts. As someone said, when American women get depressed, we go shopping! So I bought lots of clothes, stereo components, a brand-new car, a house. I was the big winner in the game show of American life, honey, they gave me ALL the doors, one, two, and three. It still wasn't enough. So I turned up the consumer volume, tuned out the real news, and read articles in women's magazines on self-improvement, hair management, techniques for makeup application, trying to buy into the lie they tell women, that my rage was internally produced, self-manufactured pain, that if I just were thinner, blonder, younger, lighter, had longer hair, bigger breasts, better clothes, stereo components, and of course, better men, had this or that, everything would be fine.

I read lots of blame-the-victim analysis by white-folks-formerly-known-as-liberal, neo-conservative Negroes, and anti-feminist feminists, strove to give them the benefit of the doubt. In the end I decided they were dangerous opportunists out for the easy American buck guaranteed to those who turn on their own. Wouldn't it be simple if racism really didn't exist, sexism either, if capitalism was benevolent and we could all do our best on the blessed level playing field of the great American meritocracy? This is not an option, there is no level playing field, and black women are at the bottom of an extremely steep incline.

I used to try and escape my rage in notions of love, sex, orgasm, but even that does not work very often anymore, my rage's appetite has grown over the years, become more specific. Now, it can only be satisfied by action, and not the pelvic kind. Vaguely, I remember a time before my rage came, or maybe there was never a time without her; we were both just younger, less wise then, inarticulate, lying back and learning the terrain, going with the flow. Way back when, I thought my rage was temporary, a tool to fight the battles, wage the struggle, win the war. Now, I understand that my rage is permanent. At worst it will drive me underground, at best it is, coupled with my hope and love, a tool. These are my trinity, forget the father, the son, and the holy ghost, they cannot help us in this black woman's world. Here, my rage and love share power, give birth to hope, they have created a fearful symmetry, a delicate balance that can keep me going or destroy me. Some days it's hard to say who's winning.

Sometimes I wish my rage would shut up, go away, leave me the hell alone, she's the conscience Jiminy Cricket sings about in Pinocchio, always there to be my guide, when I deny her my nose does not grow longer but my rage grows stronger. More and more each day though, I accept her, understand her necessity, see the ways in which she keeps me sharp, aware of and working to change this mess we're in, give birth to myself and my sisters, awake and alive.

But rage wears on your ass when you keep it all to yourself, it really does, it gets harder and harder to keep up the facade when you've got your rage to feed and manage, this is the main reason I cut my hair, besides being disgusted by the whole hair obsession and what it says about us. My hair has been short for a very long time because I just don't have the energy, inclination, or time to do hair,

the process of feeding my rage, blending it with my love, and turning them into hopeful action is too demanding. I have pretty much
given up the daily laving-on of makeup and most of the rest of the
prescribed fem bullshit. It's okay, I mean yeah, yeah, we all know
African tribes adorned themselves, et cetera, et cetera, I was a black
studies major, but it's hard to believe sisters in the bush spent hours
and big bucks applying faces to meet the faces that they'd meet, and
I know they weren't dyeing their hair blonde to look like the people who'd enslaved their neighbors, then announcing it had nothing to do with self-hatred. I am clearer, more powerful, streamlined.
What you see is what you get, a grown-up black woman fighting to
be both seen and heard.

In my forties, I have come to admit I usually feel more exhila-
rated than ashamed expressing my rage, even though, like most
women, I have been conditioned to feel it is unladylike. I grew up
with a mother who told me that girls always hold their stomachs in
and never fart in public, whose favorite adage was "Discretion is the
better part of valor," even if you ended up with permanently
clenched stomach muscles, an ulcer, and acute paranoia. Even so, she
did not mean me to be silent and invisible, just socially graceful. I
was expected to be intelligent, do well in school, go to college,
work for a living, be independent, be involved in a community of
black people, and always have money of my own. Growing up first
in my father's house and then, after his disappearance, in the house
of my mother, it never occurred to me to want or expect a man to
take care of me, I wasn't willing to pay the price of the ticket.

I have learned to control and use my rage because if I don't, it
will control and use me. This is why I gave up those things I once
used to stifle my rage, the liquor and drugs and late-night fats and
disembodied sex, universal vices, escape routes women often take to
deaden the pain, repress our frustration, suppress those niggerbitch-

fits. Turning my rage outward, I have not committed homicide or suicide because the flip side of my rage is my love, the conviction that change is possible. Still, love is hard to find, give, or receive in the culture I live in, most often when we say love what we really mean is sex, and that is more often about power and rage than love. My daughter tells me that young men her age use the term "hit it" interchangeably for fucking a woman or killing someone, and I have heard my male peers speak casually of "stabbing" a woman when what they mean is that they fucked her. And who among us wants to be the woman whose "pussy" some man "tore up" last night? Let me say I'm no fan of the word "fuck" and all its conjugations, but there's a big difference between fucking and making love and we need to be honest about which we're doing. The truth is that most of the time, in and out of bed, we're either getting fucked or fucking. These days, love is a specialty item, often out of stock. Sometimes, though, I wake up and my love is right there in bed with me, in something as simple as the sunlight coming through the window or the contrast between warm and cool as I slide my toes along the sheet. Or something truly righteous like Nelson Mandela striding out of a South African prison or deposed Surgeon General Joycelyn Elders refusing to disappear and speaking the truth—loudly—even after Clinton cut her loose in a desperate bid to save his tired self, or Congresswoman Eleanor Holmes Norton of D.C. breaking out of the male-imposed invisibility and analyzing a situation so clearly I holler with joy, or Misu making a thoughtful, independent, positive decision without consulting me, one of those "parental win" moments, when you know you did something right, or one of my friends cutting through the crap and revealing something so clear and true I'm so happy I just have to laugh. Sometimes love comes in the guise of a good man with whom I can talk and laugh, knowing that when he enters me it is not to pound out his rage but to caress me with his love, and I do the same, rage in abeyance.

If you are black and if you are female in America, love comes unexpectedly, in unexpected places, moving so fast if you don't keep your eyes wide open, you'll miss it while you're blinking. I keep my eyes open, knowing it is the love that tempers and directs the rage, the source of energy and hope that keeps me going. Without the ability to recognize and give love, I am convinced my rage would stuff my head so full the top would be blown off, they would find me dead in my chair, little bits of bone, blood, brain, and rage splattered over the ceiling and walls. I have learned that the only thing to do with my rage is recognize it, temper it with love, and blend the two together into hopeful action.

The 1980s and 90s have been devastating for many reasons, and especially for black women's demonization and erasure. We need to have a national, collective, synchronized niggerbitchfit and seize visibility, voice, and power. In the movies when it's crisis time the men are all noble, on the Titanic they're willing to drown if they must because when it comes to those lifeboats it's "women and children first." Well, at the millennium America the ship is sinking and it's black women and children first, but forget the lifeboats. More like push them overboard and if they sink silently, then roll over the other undesirables. The rhetoric of the right wing and the so-called Republican majority—so called because the real majority is the 51 percent of Americans who didn't even bother to participate in the 1996 presidential election, the lowest turnout since 1924—is first of all anti–women and children. I am reminded of this every day I hear the news and the resounding silence when it comes time for someone to speak for us. Let's face it, there is no one but us. Reagan lied about the safety nets, the brothers lied when they said they'd take care of the woman thing once they dealt with the race thing, Bill

Clinton, Newt Gingrich, Pat Buchanan, and Bob Dole lied when they said they want to "reform" welfare, many feminists are lying when they say they care about our lives. Black women have listened to these lies too long, as if wishing could make them true. We have spoken honestly about them only to each other, in our quiet, secret language, held our rage dear and pretended it didn't matter. Black women need to figure out how to weave together all our nigger-bitchfits into a collective roar of outrage and activism. Truly, we have nothing to lose. Nice white girls finish last; nice black girls don't finish at all.

What power and influence we would have if we could create a way to pull together and formalize our separate rages into the voice of the collective niggerbitchfit. Already we have informal, small, mostly passive ways in which we communicate our passions and concerns to each other. We pick up the telephone and talk to other sisters about the political silencing of outspoken black women, the Million Man March and its aftermath, the phenomena of Li'l Kim and Foxy Brown, misguided, self-hating hip hop hos as empowered black women, Clinton's impoverishment of millions of women and children when he opportunistically signed the welfare "reform" bill, the murder of Deletha Word, the destruction of the social welfare system, the attacks on our children and ourselves from in and outside our communities, the growing mean-spiritedness of America. We were saddened, but we understood the despair and profound hopelessness that led twenty-three-year-old Chicqua Roveal of Brooklyn to dress her three children in clean, warm clothes before she threw them and herself off the roof of a building. Clinging to hope, we believe that we will never go there. Still, we know it is not impossible.

Increasingly, those of us who are wired at home or at work use computers to communicate by e-mail; in minutes I can know what is bothering sisters in California, Michigan, or Alabama. In our communities we stand in the cashier's line at the grocery store and exchange information about the school board elections, the shooting last week down the block, the serial rapist whom the police have not bothered to inform us stalks our neighborhood, the crack dealers quietly establishing themselves on our streets. We communicate amongst each other about these things in that secret, quiet language of black women. But once we go home, log off, or hang up, we are again alone with our rage and often frustrated love. The challenge is how do we transform this information, these individual feelings, into collective action? How do we make ourselves and our concerns visible? What we need is to create another tongue, one that speaks for and protects all of us.

First, we must agree that we need and deserve voice, power, and influence, and this is no small task, conditioned as we are to see ourselves as less important than damn near everyone else. To be, at best, occasionally seen and even more rarely heard. We are, understandably, intimidated by the price we will be required to pay for demanding the right to define and speak for ourselves, for refusing to be the demons of opportunistic politicians, the cosmetic diversity divas of white women, the silent accomplices with black men in the lie that race, never gender, is all that matters. Some of us already know from personal experience in our homes and communities the denial, ostracism, and violence that results when we speak out. If history holds true, we know we will be further attacked and vilified, dismissed and rejected, both publicly and personally. We will suffer not only in the workplace but at home, rejected by patriarchs and patriarchal aspirants on both fronts. That is the price of taking voice. But the potential rewards, once gained, are tremendous. United we will be able to affect what happens to us, and to influence what goes on in our homes, our communities, and our nation.

On a daily basis we will be able to communicate locally, nationally, and internationally about what is or should be of concern to us: the fact that as black women we are most likely to raise our children alone and in poverty, that the rate of black women who are incarcerated is increasing faster than any other population, that the number of women who are victims of violent crimes, especially among poor women, is steadily growing, that the face of AIDS is becoming increasingly black, brown, and female, that three-quarters of all rapes and assaults against women are committed by men we know. That not only in America, but wherever we are in the world, black women do most of the work in our communities but have the least amount of money and power. Is it any wonder that, according to a study by the Center for Health Statistics released in the spring of 1997, black women are the unhappiest people in America? The tragedy is that while the real conditions in which we live worsen, we simultaneously become more disdained and less visible to others. It is up to us to recognize that the list of our concerns is large and ever-growing. So should be our voice.

We have no alternative, unless we choose erasure and invisibility, consign ourselves to remain ghosts and specters. Over time, denied the affirmation of self-definition and visibility, many of us lose all sense of our own selves and substance. Whatever scraps of ourselves we encounter in the larger culture will continue to be determined by the needs of others. A few of us will be allowed to be Mammy, or The Tragic Widow, or Demonized Welfare Cheat, or Nationalist Queen for a Day. A few more will be briefly visible as objectified sexual beings, objects of the sexual and racial fantasies of men, visible in high heels, short skirts, long, store-bought hair, red lips, protruding buttocks, lingerie as clothing, preferably all of the above. We will be seen because we are objects of sexual desire and submission, for no other reason, and with that troubled visibility will come the threat of exploitation and violence. As we get older, even this will fade. Some of us will attempt to escape this fate by becoming middle class, surrounding ourselves with brand-name purchases, marrying a professional man, producing the requisite number of children, pretending that the erasure and violence that surrounds us does not exist, or at least cannot touch us. But the truth is that for the overwhelming majority of black women even these pitiful delaying tactics will not work, we will remain unseen and unheard and victimized, continue to quietly go about the business of helping others survive, doing most of the work in our communities, and barely surviving ourselves, silently. All of us will continue to have our lonely niggerbitchfits, inflicting our rage and pain most of all on ourselves.

Whichever of these lousy choices we make, what lies down the road of being defined by others, remaining powerless and voiceless, inevitably, is increased invisibility, because eventually we will have outlived our usefulness to black men as malleable icons, or to politicians as convenient whipping girls, or to boys and men as sexual receptacles and fantasies. Even if we mask ourselves so that men will not see who we are, but who they want us to be, we will fail in the end. Because we will all inevitably become, whether we choose to, whether we like it or not, and even whether we know it, grown-up black women. Then, if we have not figured out a way to create a consciousness for black women that speaks for and to us, a way to seize power, we will fade from view, disappear, having staked out no independent definition and use for ourselves.

My mother, the certified Red Cross lifeguard from Indiana, taught me how to swim when I was a little girl. I have been swimming ever since, always with her voice in my ear, a few words of instruction for each stroke, the backstroke with its "UpOutDown," the sidestroke, "ReachOpenClose," the perilous and hard to master breast stroke, "StrokeDownBreathe, StrokeDownBreathe." I hear my mother always, most clearly when I am swimming. In water I glide along, confident and powerful, in control because I know the strokes. Her words surround me. Even as I try to shut them out, resist being the dutiful daughter, the obedient one, I am caught in the sea of her voice, her instruction. There is not a shred of doubt in my mind that if I do not obey I will surely sink like a rock, the sea of the world will close green-blue and silent just above my head, and I will drown. Occasionally, I break the surface, dive deep, but always come up for air, sometimes shaken, sputtering, but never drowned. Only graceless people who don't know the strokes disappear in a sea of salt or love or rage.

As a girl, I swam because my mother made me. Nowadays, I swim to stay afloat and get where I want to go, do most of my swimming on dry land. Childhood fear of the cold and of the unknown, whatever monsters might lurk beneath the surface, was no excuse with my mother. Neither was remaining in a depth I could stand in, touching bottom. The four of us would learn to swim, not only because swimming was fun and good exercise, it was a family trait, a Ransom virtue on my mother's side, she and her five brothers were all swimmers, a Nelson virtue by dint of the fact that being excellent swimmers fit into my father's mantra of being the best, number one. Swimming was a point of honor, the grace of our strokes as much an inherited trait as big thighs or big egos. Years later, when I am an adult woman swimming laps, a man stops and asks if I am my mother's daughter. I tell him yes, then ask how he knew. "Well, there's some physical resemblance, though you're bigger," he says. "But you swim exactly like her, same stroke."

My mother taught me how to swim, how to breathe, to stay afloat, enough to be able to survive, move forward, excel, but not enough to enable me to escape the pull of the current, the undertow, the treacherous spots. How to translate her admonitions—"Don't swim out too far," "Stay away from the current around the jetties," "Never swim out after a beach ball blown by the wind"—to work, love, politics, friendship, family, to life? Until recently, I was angry with my mother, thought she had shortchanged me, failed, abdicated her motherly responsibility in teaching me just enough, not all. A mother myself now, I know that it is both impossible and inappropriate to teach your children both how to swim and what direction to go in. Usually when people try to do that their children are weak swimmers lacking a sense of purpose. Years of therapy, both the fifty-minute hour and the equally important kind that takes place over the telephone with women friends who at times I trust more than myself, have taught me that this is just the way it is, my mother did the best she could. I've learned that no one, not even Mommy, can give you the really hard shit, you have to get that all by yourself.

Thanks to my mother, I know I will not vanish in the ocean, or lake, or pool, or the sea. If the current pulls me out, I can swim parallel to it, surrender, float, lie on my back and go with the flow. Once out of its clutches I can head back toward solid ground with a graceful breast stroke. If I tire, I can flip onto my back and into my backstroke, UpOutDown, UpOutDown toward solid ground. My mother taught me how to swim, but not which direction to swim in, or who to swim alongside, not how to navigate. Now that I am a grown-up black woman, I have to figure that out for myself.

I never met Deletha Word, have only seen one photograph of her, the same image over and over in newspapers, magazines, on television, a posed shot of a brown-skinned woman with an elaborate, just-from-the-beauty-parlor hairstyle and a sweet, eager smile. We never met, but I know her. If we'd passed on the street, if our eyes met, I would surely have recognized in the tilt of her head, set of her lips, stride of her legs, the same things I see in my own mirror. Black women, we live similar lives, speak the same language. Once upon a time, I thought I was alone, and invisible, and crazy. I searched outside myself and my sisters for escape from the rage, pain, and invisibility of being black and female in America. In the process of becoming a grown-up black woman I have learned that the only escape route is to come together, find our voice, take action. It's time for all of us, on a sinking ship and remembering Deletha Word, to learn how to swim.

I USED TO HATE THE DAY when report cards came, not because my grades were low but because even when I got A's and B's, in the space for comments my teachers would inevitably write, "Jill is not living up to her potential." In a weird way, I wanted to be either without potential or a kid who got all C's and next to them the teacher scrawled, "Good work!" It is not until I am grown that I understand this classmate does not exist, that if there is one thing we all share it is the potential to do better, reach more distant goals. Even knowing this, old habits die hard.

It is only recently that I have been able to admit to myself that even though I never liked dolls and have known for a very long time that for the most part I exist outside the culture, some secret part of me still thought I had a shot at being Barbie. Not literally. I'm long past coveting hair, or skinniness, or rock-hard perky breasts, and I never wanted to be white. Still, I thought it was possible to be independent, outspoken, and adversarial most of the time, and then when it was convenient switch over into being none of these things, become a pretty, silent airhead, spiffily dressed, strolling hand in hand with my Afro Ken. Now I know that this is not possible, that once on the road to self-definition, voice, and visibility, there are detours, but no turning back, no way to pretend I do not know, feel, and see myself and what is around me. This is the price I pay for no longer feeling alone, or invisible, or crazy. I still have occasional pungent moments of wanting to tune out, front myself off, moments of Barbie yearning. The good news is that as time goes on these moments are fewer.

What is constantly on my mind is how I learn more about what it does, can, and should mean to be a grown-up black woman, not just for myself, but for my sisters, brothers, and everyone else. I am convinced that black women can and must be a powerful voice in the local, national, and international dialogue, that we are a crucial part of transforming the culture into one that is safe for all of us. Once we know what the problems and challenges are, the question is how most effectively to take action.

The work that we have to do is both internal and external. What bothers me about many of the self-help, spiritual uplift, know thyself, meditation books on the market, books that are extremely successful and marketed specifically to women, is that more often than not they suggest that the work to be done is solely or largely internal, as if the problems that confront women are primarily self-created. Too often, the subtext of these books is "Get yourself together and everything will be all right." Nothing could be further from the truth. You can read spiritual adages, meditate, and work on yourself twenty-two hours a day, but during those two hours when you have to go outside and interact with others you will inevitably be bombarded by the values and violence of the society in which we live. It's crucial to be clear that the work is both internal and external. The challenge is to get ourselves together and simultaneously engage in external activism. The time that we spend overtly engaged in the internal work of knowing and improving ourselves serves to fuel and drive our engagement with the external world of community, work, and the nation. At the same time, the external work we do tests, expands, and puts into action the things we learn and believe.

Most important is that as black women we get actively involved, both with ourselves and the world outside ourselves, declare ourselves important players. What follows are some suggestions for how to get started that work for me. If you don't relate to them, cool. Create your own. The thing not to do is nothing. That's the same as erasing yourself.

1. Schedule time to spend with yourself. In this way you declare yourself important, place yourself at the center. If you don't, why should anyone else? I exercise an hour a day. That hour swimming, running, or lifting weights is a meditative time for me. I spend it thinking about everything and nothing, but every day I feel smarter, calmer, and clearer. This isn't a workout book, and I'm not pushing exercise. It doesn't matter what you do. Meditate, sit in your favorite chair, pray, take a walk, listen to music, as long as you make time for yourself.

2. Learn how to look at culture critically. We're all raised to be cultural consumers and absorb what's around us passively, like sponges. This makes many black women feel inadequate, enraged, or crazy. Make the effort to see independent films, read history, criticism, nonfiction, and get information from outside mainstream media. The proliferation of black

women's book clubs, in which groups of women meet regularly—usually in someone's apartment with a potluck dinner—to discuss books they've read, is another good route. So are lectures and seminars in schools, churches, and community-based organizations that are usually free, open to the public, and encourage discussion.

Understand that the personal is political, the political personal. When you watch television, flip through a magazine, see a movie or an art exhibit, don't fool yourself that you're simply being passively entertained. Ask yourself questions. Some of mine are: How were black women and black people portrayed? What was presented as "normal" and what as "abnormal"? What was the political agenda? Do I feel dissed and assaulted or challenged and affirmed by the work? Talk back to those who portray us negatively. Don't take misrepresentation passively.

3. Make time to spend with a group of black women where you talk about yourselves, and not in terms of anyone else. Think about how much time women spend talking about men, or children, or the job, and how little we talk about ourselves and each other, who we are and who we'd like to be. The first step to sisterhood and forming a collective identity as black women is to talk honestly about and amongst ourselves.

4. Learn about feminism. We've all been manipulated and scared off by the word, but get over it. The simple definition of feminism is the theory of the political, economic, and social equality of the sexes. Period. Hard to argue with that. If you have a problem with the word, find another one. The im-

portant thing is to believe and act in ways that support your right to equality. Read the work of black women writers on the subject.

5. Get involved in your local community. We've become so alienated from each other that we have lost the basis of what community is, individuals interacting with each other for the betterment of all. I know we're all busy as hell, but on the real side we manage to find time to run our mouths on the telephone, stare at bad television, or be depressed, time that could be better spent building community. The knowledge that you are powerful and can effect change grows out of involvement with your community. Volunteer at a community-based organization, religious institution, or community center. Join the food co-op, tutor students, coach sports, help the elderly, organize your neighbors for street beautification, crime watch, plant a community garden.

6. Speak. Or at least nod. One of the nicest things about the 1960s and early 1970s was that black people made eye contact, said good morning, spoke to one another. Nowadays, meeting someone's eye is seen as a threat. Speaking is a way of acknowledging all of our visibility. It serves to reaffirm our connection as women, men, a people, and humans. That connection is what community is about. Speak to white folks. They need it, too. Home training, as we all know, comes through black women.

7. Think about politics from a self-interested perspective. Then do something. Bad as the political scene is, it's dangerous denial to pretend it doesn't affect all of our lives. From the

current move by Christian fundamentalists to take over local school boards across America, to the control of the House and Senate by the right, to the increasingly backward decisions of the Supreme Court, to the national increase of violence against women, we're all affected. Whatever your party or personal politics, whether you participate in elections or your agenda is the establishment of an independent black homeland, do something. If you don't, you're not cool, a superior jaded intellectual, or in the vanguard, you're a victim.

8. Ask for, and offer, help. Forget the super-black-woman-who-can-do-everything-including-squat-in-the-field-birth-a-baby-and-keep-on-pickin'-dat-cotton stereotype. Knowing you need help and asking for it is the first step in solving problems. So is recognizing that other women need support and offering it. Assistance can range from something as simple as taking a friend's children for a day before she has a nigger-bitchfit on them, to volunteering for a local candidate, to going on the Internet to ask a nation of wired black women for support and counsel, to asking a friend to refer you to a therapist. Reach out instead of doing what we usually do when we need help, which is to deny it and do even more until we go into crisis and collapse.

9. Don't compare yourself out. Don't look around for sisters you can feel superior to, then use them to make yourself feel better and justify remaining exactly where you are. Women in search of visibility, voice, and a place at the table are linked, whatever our age, class, physical attributes, job, color, or geographical location. We need to remember this and ap-

proach each other with love, acceptance, and active support. This is an important step in creating a collective consciousness.

10. Recognize, understand, and put your rage to use. Take that negative, internalized niggerbitchfit and use it to work toward positive internal and external change. Imagine how powerful we would be, what we could accomplish, if black women across the country were communicating and organizing. Reach out to black women where you find them.

Sisters! Come out, come out! Wherever you are.

Let me hear your voice. Please E-mail me at Straightnochaser@ngn.net or write me c/o Putnam Penguin Inc., 200 Madison Avenue, New York, NY 10016.